P9-BZZ-812

The Soufflé Cookbook

Myra Waldo

Dover Publications, Inc., *New York*

Published in Canada by General Publishing Company, Ltd., 30 Lesmill Road, Don Mills, Toronto, Ontario.
Published in the United Kingdom by Constable and Company, Ltd., 10 Orange Street, London WC2H 7EG.

This Dover edition, first published in 1990, is a republication of the work originally published by Thomas Y. Crowell Company, N.Y., in 1954 with the title *Serve at Once: The Soufflé Cookbook*. A few corrections and adjustments have been made tacitly in the text. Nine recipes calling for the ingredient Sucaryl have been deleted from the chapter "Low-Calorie Soufflés."

Manufactured in the United States of America.
Dover Publications, Inc., 31 East 2nd Street, Mineola, N.Y. 11501

Library of Congress Cataloging-in-Publication Data

Waldo, Myra.
The soufflé cookbook / Myra Waldo.
p. cm.
Reprint. Originally published: Serve at once: the soufflé cookbook. New York : T.Y. Crowell, 1954
ISBN 0-486-26416-5
1. Soufflés. I. Waldo, Myra. Serve at once: the soufflé cookbook. II. Title.
TX773.W3 1990
641.8′2—dc20 90-33320
CIP

Contents

ONE

How to Make a Perfect Soufflé

The one dish that invariably excites both the appetite and the imagination is the soufflé. Perfectly prepared, properly presented, it is one of the high points of culinary art.

Most people assume that soufflé preparation is beyond their abilities. This is not true, for while the making requires a certain amount of skill, it can be mastered by anyone who can cook even simple dishes.

Primarily, the nature of a soufflé must be understood. It is customarily described as "a dish which, when baked in the oven, expands considerably, usually because of a quantity of egg whites contained in the recipe." Of course, this is only a general description, because soufflé recipes vary. However, the main points to remember are that a soufflé rises when it is placed in the oven, a soufflé is delicate, and it should be eaten as soon as it comes out of oven and is brought to the table.

Let us suppose that we have prepared a mixture as called for in the recipe and, for example, have stirred together, until very smooth, flour, butter, milk, and various other ingredients. It is absolutely essential that this mixture be as smooth as you can make it. If there are lumps or other undissolved particles, the soufflé mixture cannot rise evenly. The mixture should be cool when the egg whites are added.

The egg whites should be prepared with care, for it is upon this operation that the success or failure of a soufflé largely depends. The egg whites should be at room temperature before beating, so remove eggs from the refrigerator sufficiently ahead of time to allow them to reach room temperature. Place the whites in a rather large bowl. An electric mixer, hand-held rotary beater, or a wire whisk may be used. However, a high-speed electric blender is not advisable.

How long to beat the whites? Actually, there is no way to tell except by examination of the whites as the beating continues. As you beat them, you will notice a gradual thickening. Next, there will be a foaminess with bubbles flying about. At this point you must beat with care, for the next stage, when the whites are stiff but not dry, is the desired one. This point is reached when the whites hold their shape and stand in peaks, even though you have stopped beating them. If you continue to whip them, they will hold their shape, but will become dry; that is, they will lose their air bubbles. Beat egg whites only until stiff—*but not dry.*

Now we are ready to fold the whites into the previously prepared mixture, which has been placed in a fairly large bowl. It is best to use a large wooden spoon to fold in the beaten whites, since by using this type of spoon you will be less likely to break down the air cells in the egg whites. The success or failure of your soufflé will be determined largely by how you incorporate the whites into the soufflé mixture.

Take approximately half of the beaten whites and spoon them

onto the soufflé mixture. Stir thoroughly, but *slowly* and lightly. This should take not longer than 1 minute. Now, take the remaining half of the beaten whites and add them *very gently* to the other mixture, folding them in *carefully* and lightly, for not more than 15 or 20 seconds. There may be patches of egg whites showing at the end of this time, but they are unimportant and will not affect the result. Use the wooden spoon as lightly and gently as possible, working it slowly in an up-and-down circular motion, as illustrated:

The combining of the stiffly-beaten egg whites with the soufflé mixture is not complicated, providing the instructions are followed. Here they are summarized:

1. Beat the egg whites until stiff, but not dry.

2. Place half of the whites on the soufflé mixture and stir in with a wooden spoon very lightly and slowly for not more than 1 minute.

3. Add the balance of the whites and fold them in lightly and

slowly for 15 to 20 seconds, disregarding any white patches that may remain.

The purpose of all this is to incorporate as many air bubbles as possible, and also to make them as large as possible. When placed in the oven, these air spaces will become heated. Because hot air rises, the soufflé will expand. Just as hot air expands, so does cold air contract; and if we allow any cold air or drafts to hit the soufflé while it is baking, it will shrink and fall.

The proper size and shape for an oven soufflé dish varies according to the ingredients used. However, it may generally be stated that a 4-egg soufflé is best baked in a dish with a 1½-quart (6-cup) capacity; a 6-egg soufflé is best baked in a 2-quart (8-cup) dish.

The ideal soufflé dish is made of either ovenproof glass or pottery. The sides should be as straight as possible. Examples of good soufflé dishes are shown in the illustrations.

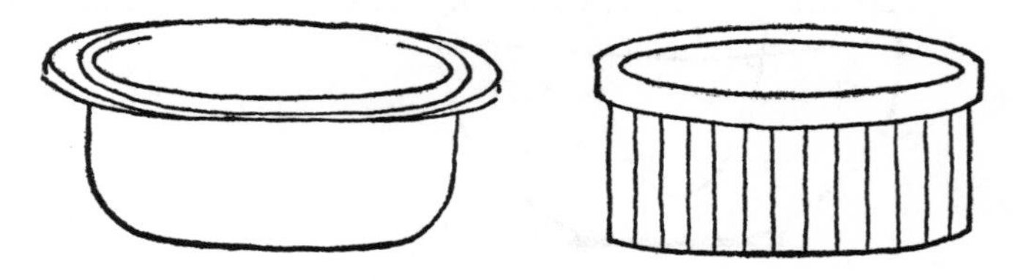

The straight-side dish permits the soufflé to rise to its maximum height, and look like this:

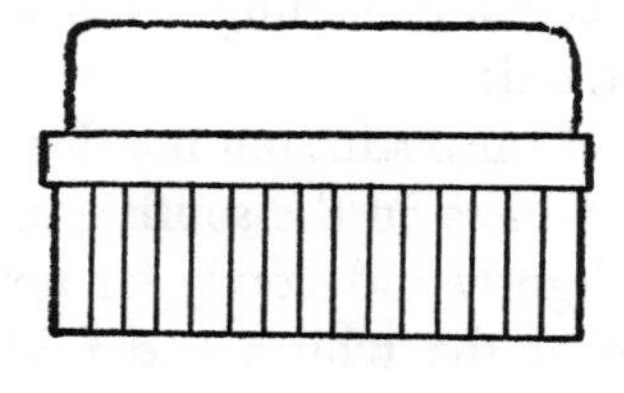

However, a dish with slightly sloping sides may be used. The resulting soufflé will rise somewhat differently:

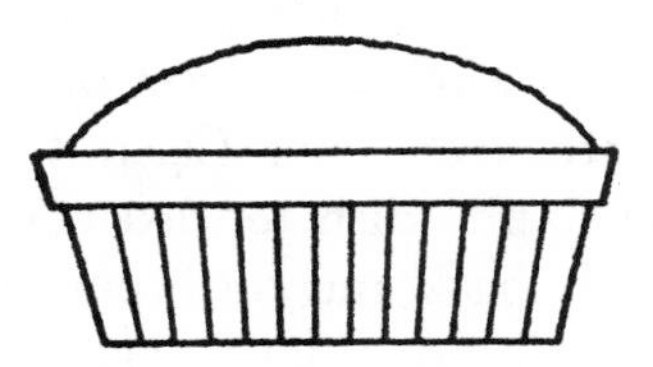

You will note that some of the recipes require a buttered soufflé dish, whereas others do not. Whenever possible, the baking dish should not be greased, because that makes the sides of the dish slippery, thus making it easier for the soufflé to fall when it is removed from the oven. In some soufflés, however, the nature of the mixture requires a buttered dish, or buttering and sprinkling with flour, sugar, or bread crumbs. These latter ingredients help to make the sides of the dish less slippery.

Do not peep into the oven to see if the soufflé has risen properly until 5 minutes before the end of the specified baking time. Opening the oven door admits cool air, often enough to collapse the soufflé unless it is nearly done.

What is happening in the oven is this: As the air cells in the mixture expand, the soufflé mixture is forced to expand. If this expansion holds steady during the first part of the baking time, the soufflé cooks to a gentle firmness and holds its shape even after it is removed from the oven. If cold air hits the soufflé mixture before it has become sufficiently firm, the air cells contract, and the soufflé falls.

Ovens vary greatly; even the most modern, with a thermostat, is not always accurate. To check your oven, place an oven thermometer on the baking rack and compare the thermometer and the oven regulator temperatures. Because of this possible variance, the baking times specified in the recipes can be only approximate, but they should not vary by more than 5 minutes.

Thus, when you come to the last 5 minutes of baking time, an inspection is in order. The kitchen window or outside door should be closed when you open the oven door. Open it slowly, and do not let it slam shut. Pull the soufflé dish toward you gently, using a pot-holder. Move it carefully back and forth once or twice to see if the mixture is set. Do not insert a knife or toothpick, for this will permit the warm air in the soufflé to escape. Rather, learn by observation. If the soufflé is done, the top will be a golden brown with a very light crust. In a completely baked soufflé, the mixture will not shake when moved back and forth. If it does not meet these requirements, it undoubtedly needs a little longer baking.

In France, it is the custom to eat a soufflé when it is quite moist inside, using the partially cooked interior as a sauce. However, the American taste is for a more firmly baked soufflé, and the baking time in these recipes has been worked out to meet that taste. If you prefer a wetter soufflé, merely deduct a few minutes from the specified baking time. Overcooking, however, will toughen a soufflé.

Have your guests at the table, ready to eat the soufflé; a soufflé will not await the guests. Have ready on the table the warmed plates, a serving spoon, the sauce for the soufflé (if it is called for), and, of course, a plate or trivet to hold the hot soufflé dish.

The delight of the beholders in seeing the perfectly risen soufflé will be reward enough for your efforts. There is apparently no other dish that pleases the guest as does a soufflé—the ultimate in cookery!

And always remember, Serve at once!

For successful results, keep in mind the following important points:

If you have never made a soufflé before, try making one for yourself and your family, not for guests.

Fill the soufflé dish about three-quarters full unless otherwise specified in the recipe.

If the quantity of the recipe exceeds the capacity of your soufflé dish, first put a buttered paper collar around the outside edge of the dish and tie it in place. (This is described in detail in the introduction to the section on Cold Soufflés.) If this is done, the dish may be filled to its capacity or even slightly more, and the paper collar will protect the soufflé when it rises. A dramatic effect is achieved this way, as the soufflé will rise inside the collar considerably over the top of the dish.

You can prepare the mixture in advance, except the egg whites. The egg whites must be beaten just before they are added to the mixture. The whole must then be placed in the oven immediately. Never allow a soufflé mixture to stand after adding the egg whites.

An extra egg white or two, in addition to those called for in the recipe, will make the soufflé lighter and increase its rising power.

Hot ingredients or mixtures may be cooled more rapidly by placing them on ice or in the refrigerator. This will usually cut the cooling time in half.

Where a recipe specifies "stirring constantly," it means just that. This is especially important when combining butter, flour, and milk over low heat; failure to stir constantly will result in a lumpy white sauce. If lumps do form, they may be removed only by pressing the white sauce through a fine strainer.

Liquor of any sort, but especially brandy, aids in the rising process of a soufflé. You may safely add 2 tablespoons of brandy to any recipe to assist in the baking process. No alcohol remains in the finished soufflé. Unless otherwise specified, the brandy called for in these recipes is of the cognac type, rather than the fruit liqueurs.

It is possible to prepare a soufflé that may be held in the oven for about 15 minutes beyond the normal baking time. The resulting soufflé will not be so delicate in flavor or texture as normally, and this method is suggested only for those situations in which you anticipate an emergency. (The only dessert soufflés in which this method is applicable are the chocolate soufflés.) To the beaten egg whites, add 2 teaspoons of cream of tartar and 2 teaspoons of white or cider vinegar. Beat for an additional 30 seconds, then proceed as directed in the recipe. At the end of the specified baking time, reduce the oven temperature to the lowest possible point. The soufflé will hold for an additional 15 minutes or so, although it will get somewhat brown on top.

If you want to serve a larger number of people than the recipe specifies, double the recipe, but use two soufflé dishes; don't use one larger dish. Never use a soufflé dish larger than a 2-quart (8-cup) size. If a larger size is used, the soufflé will not bake properly. Place the soufflé dish in the center of the oven.

Be sure the soufflé dish and all mixing bowls that you use are completely dry. The presence of additional water may affect the rising of the soufflé.

Where a recipe is specified as yielding 2 to 4 servings, the assumption is that the dish yields only 2 servings if the soufflé constitutes the main part of the meal; it will be sufficient for 4 servings if the soufflé is to be only one course of the meal.

For an unusual effect, make a soufflé with a "top hat." When the mixture has been poured into the soufflé dish, and before it is placed in the oven, run the handle of a table knife around the mixture about 1½ inches from the outside edge. Hold the knife so that the handle is about 1 to 2 inches deep in the mixture and make a complete circle, being sure to stay 1½ inches from the side of the dish. Place the soufflé in the oven at once. It will usually rise more in the center than on the outside, creating the top hat effect.

It is never advisable to have two soufflés in the same meal, as, for example, a meat soufflé and a dessert soufflé. Combine a crunchy food, such as a green salad, with the soft texture of a main-dish soufflé.

TWO

Appetizer and Fish Soufflés

The idea of an appetizer soufflé is comparatively unknown in this country. The opposite is true in Europe, particularly in France. In that country, a soufflé may appear at any stage of the meal.

It is a novel beginning to any dinner to serve a soufflé as the first course, and a fish soufflé is particularly appropriate for this. With or without a maid, a first-course soufflé is readily prepared. The trick is to have the soufflé mixture ready, with the exception of egg whites. While the guests are having a predinner drink, beat the egg whites, and fold them into the soufflé mixture. Place in the oven as described in the recipe. Approximately 30 minutes (or whatever time is specified) later, your guests can go to the table, and your first-course soufflé can come in immediately afterward.

Most of the recipes in this chapter will serve four persons as an appetizer or first course of a meal. If the soufflé is to be eaten as a main course, the recipe will be enough for only two or three people.

Clam Soufflé

[4 servings]

3 tbsp. butter
1 tbsp. grated onion
2 tbsp. cornstarch
¾ cup clam juice
¾ cup light cream, scalded
1 tsp. salt
¼ tsp. pepper
4 egg yokes, beaten
1 can minced clams, *or* 18 small fresh clams, chopped and drained
5 egg whites

Melt the butter in a saucepan, add the onion and sauté lightly 2 minutes.

Add cornstarch, mixing well. Add clam juice and cream, stirring constantly. Cook 10 minutes over low heat, stirring occasionally. Add salt and pepper.

Remove from the heat and beat this mixture very slowly into the egg yolks. Stir constantly to prevent curdling. Allow to cool for 10 minutes.

Add the chopped and drained clams to the first mixture. Preheat oven to moderate, 350°F.

Beat the egg whites until stiff but not dry. Fold into the clam mixture carefully. Pour mixture into an unbuttered 1½-quart soufflé dish. Bake 35 minutes.

Serve at once.

Crab-Meat Soufflé

[4 servings]

4 tbsp. butter
3 tbsp. sifted all-purpose flour
1 cup milk, scalded
1 cup cooked or canned crab meat, shredded
1 tbsp. sherry or Madeira
1 tbsp. lemon juice
1 tsp. salt
½ tsp. pepper
dash cayenne pepper
4 egg yolks, beaten
5 egg whites

Melt the butter in a saucepan, add flour, and stir until smooth. Slowly add milk, stirring constantly. Cook over low heat, until thick and smooth, about 5 minutes. Add crab meat, wine, lemon juice, salt, pepper, and cayenne. Mix well, and let cool for 5 minutes.

Add the egg yolks gradually, stirring constantly to prevent curdling. Set aside to cool for at least 15 minutes. Preheat oven to moderate, 350°F.

Beat the egg whites until stiff but not dry. Fold into the yolk mixture carefully. Pour into an unbuttered 1½-quart soufflé dish. Bake 35 minutes.

Serve at once.

Individual Crab-Meat Soufflés

[4 servings]

1 cup cooked or canned crab meat
2 tbsp. sherry
3 tbsp. butter
5 tbsp. sifted all-purpose flour
1 cup milk, scalded
½ cup clam juice
¼ cup sliced, stuffed green olives
1 tsp. salt
3 egg yolks, beaten
3 egg whites
dash cayenne pepper

Flake the crab meat, and pour sherry over it. Mix and let marinate in the wine.

Melt butter in a saucepan, add the flour, and mix well. Slowly add the milk and then the clam juice, stirring constantly. Cook until smooth and thick, about 5 minutes. Add the crab meat, olives, and salt, and let cool 5 minutes. Add the egg yolks, and mix well. Preheat oven to moderate, 350°F.

Beat the egg whites until stiff but not dry. Fold into crab mixture carefully. Pour into four 1½-cup buttered soufflé dishes and sprinkle cayenne pepper on top of each. Bake 15 minutes.

Serve at once.

Finnan Haddie Soufflé

[4 servings]

4 tbsp. butter
1 onion, peeled and chopped
¼ cup sifted all-purpose flour
2 cups stock, *or* 2 cups boiling water and 2 chicken bouillon cubes
2 tsp. curry powder
3 tbsp. sherry
1½ pounds finnan haddie
3 egg yolks, beaten
2 pimientos, chopped
1 tbsp. chopped parsley
3 egg whites

Melt the butter in a saucepan, add onion, and sauté 2 minutes. Add flour and mix until smooth. Add the stock, stirring constantly. Cook 10 minutes longer, or until the mixture is reduced to about 1½ cups. Add curry powder and sherry and strain. Set aside to cool for 20 minutes.

Rinse the finnan haddie, and soak in a bowl of warm water 20 minutes. Drain carefully, rinse, drain again. Grind the fish in a meat grinder or food chopper. Add the egg yolks gradually to the cooled cream sauce, beating well. Add the ground fish, pimientos and parsley. Mix all together thoroughly. Preheat oven to moderate, 375°F.

Beat the egg whites until stiff but not dry. Fold into the fish mixture carefully. Pour into an unbuttered 1½-quart soufflé dish. Bake 35 minutes.

Serve at once.

This soufflé may be served with White Wine Sauce, see page 223.

Fish-Ball Soufflé

[4 servings]

- 4 tbsp. butter
- ¼ cup sifted all-purpose flour
- ¾ cup milk, scalded
- ¾ cup heavy cream, scalded
- 1 tsp. salt
- ½ tsp. pepper
- 3 egg yolks, beaten
- 1 cup cooked white-meat fish
- 1 tsp. lemon juice
- 2 tbsp. grated onion
- 8 cooked shrimp, cleaned and chopped
- 3 egg whites
- 4 tbsp. bread crumbs

Melt the butter in a saucepan, add flour, and stir until smooth. Add milk and cream, stirring constantly. Add salt and pepper, cooking until smooth and thick, about 5 minutes, stirring constantly. Let cool for 5 minutes. Add egg yolks gradually, stirring constantly. Set aside to cool.

Grind the cooked fish fine in a food mill or grinder; add 3 tablespoons of the egg mixture to the fish. Add lemon juice and onion, and mix well together. Correct seasoning. Shape into small balls about 1 inch in diameter. Set aside.

Butter a 2-quart soufflé dish well, and dust with the bread crumbs. Place the fish balls in the bottom.

Add the chopped shrimp to the cream sauce and egg mixture, and mix well. Preheat oven to moderate, 375°F.

Beat the egg whites until stiff but not dry. Fold into the shrimp mixture carefully. Pour the soufflé mixture over the fish balls in the soufflé dish. Bake 25 minutes.

Serve at once.

This soufflé may be served with Mushroom Sauce, see page 221.

Fish Soufflé

[4 servings]

1 tbsp. butter
1 tbsp. chopped onion
¼ cup white wine
½ pound fillets uncooked white-meat fish
½ tsp. salt
¼ tsp. pepper

Melt the butter in a saucepan, add onion and wine. Place the fish in the pan, add salt and pepper, and cook over moderate heat 20 minutes. Press the fish through a food mill and set aside to cool. Prepare the following:

3 tbsp. butter
2½ tbsp. sifted all-purpose flour
1½ cups milk, scalded
3 egg yolks
4 egg whites

Melt the butter in a saucepan, add the flour, and stir until smooth. Add milk, stirring constantly; continue cooking about 10 minutes over low heat; stir occasionally. Add the ground fish, and stir well. Remove from heat, and let cool 10 minutes. Beat the egg yolks until light in color; gradually add them to the fish mixture, beating constantly. Preheat oven to moderate, 350°F.

Beat the egg whites until stiff but not dry. Fold into the previous mixture carefully. Pour into a buttered 1½-quart soufflé dish. Bake 35 minutes.

Serve at once.

Curried Fish-and-Apple Soufflé

[4 servings]

- 5 tbsp. butter
- ½ cup finely chopped onion
- 1 cup cubed pared apple
- 2 tbsp. sifted all-purpose flour
- 2 tbsp. curry powder
- ½ tsp. salt
- 1 cup milk, scalded
- 2 tbsp. finely chopped parsley
- 1 clove garlic, minced
- 4 egg yolks, beaten
- 1 cup finely ground cooked fish
- 4 egg whites

Melt 3 tablespoons of the butter in a saucepan; add the onion and apple. Cook over low heat until the apple is soft, about 5 to 10 minutes.

Melt the remaining 2 tablespoons of butter in another saucepan. Add the flour, curry powder, and salt. Stir until smooth. Gradually add the milk, stirring constantly until the boiling point is reached. Add parsley and garlic. Cook 5 minutes, stirring occasionally. Combine with onion-apple mixture. Mix well. Let cool 10 minutes, then add the egg yolks, beating well. Add the fish carefully. Correct the seasoning. Preheat oven to moderate, 350°F.

Beat the egg whites until stiff but not dry. Fold into fish mixture carefully. Pour into four buttered individual 1½-cup soufflé dishes. Bake 20 minutes.

Serve at once.

Fish-Ring Soufflé

[4 servings]

1 pound white-meat fish, uncooked
2 tbsp. lemon juice
1 cup water
1 cup heavy cream
1 cup soft bread crumbs
2 tbsp. vermouth
1 tsp. salt
¼ tsp. pepper
4 egg whites

Soak the fish in lemon juice and water 10 minutes. Drain, and discard the liquid. Remove the skin and bones carefully. Grind the fish fine in a food grinder.

Combine the cream and bread crumbs, reserving 1 tablespoon of crumbs; let crumbs soak in the cream a few minutes. Add the fish and mix well. Add vermouth, salt, and pepper. Mix together, and then correct seasoning.

Butter a 7-inch ring mold, and dust with the remaining tablespoon of bread crumbs. Preheat oven to moderate, 350°F.

Beat the egg whites until stiff but not dry; carefully fold them into the fish. Pour the soufflé into the mold and place the mold in a shallow pan of hot water. Bake 45 minutes.

When ready, run a knife around the edge of the mold, tap gently on all sides, and turn out carefully onto a warmed plate.

Serve at once.

The center may be filled with Mushroom-Almond Sauce, see page 221.

Kipper Soufflé

[4 servings]

2 tbsp. olive oil
1 clove garlic, minced
1 onion, peeled and chopped
3 tomatoes, peeled and sliced
2 (3½-oz.) cans kipper snacks, flaked
3 tbsp. butter
¼ cup sifted all-purpose flour
1 cup milk, scalded
½ tsp. salt
¼ tsp. pepper
½ tsp. dry mustard
2 tbsp. grated Parmesan cheese
4 egg yolks, beaten
4 egg whites

Heat olive oil in a saucepan; add garlic and onion; sauté 2 minutes. Add the tomatoes, and cook 3 minutes. Add kippers, mix lightly, and set aside.

Melt butter in another pan, add flour, stir until smooth. Gradually add the milk, stirring constantly until the boiling point is reached. Cook over low heat 5 minutes, stirring occasionally. Add salt, pepper, mustard, and cheese. Mix well. Combine with kipper mixture. Let cool for 10 minutes. Add the egg yolks, beating constantly. Preheat oven to moderate, 350°F.

Beat the egg whites until stiff but not dry. Fold into kipper mixture carefully. Pour into an unbuttered 1½-quart soufflé dish. Bake 30 minutes.

Serve at once.

Lobster-Curry Soufflé

[4 servings]

- 3 tbsp. butter
- 1 onion, peeled and grated
- 1 clove garlic, crushed
- 3 tbsp. sifted all-purpose flour
- ¼ tsp. powdered ginger
- 2 tsp. curry powder
- 1 cup light cream, scalded
- 2 cups sliced cooked lobster meat
- 2 tsp. parsley
- 3 egg yolks, beaten
- 3 egg whites
- 2 tbsp. ground blanched almonds

Melt the butter in a saucepan, add onion and garlic, and sauté 2 minutes over low heat, stirring occasionally. Add the flour and stir until very smooth. Add the ginger and curry powder. Slowly add cream, stirring constantly. Bring to a boil and let simmer 3 minutes, stirring occasionally. Add lobster, parsley, and egg yolks, stirring all together very well. Let cool. Correct the seasoning. A little additional curry powder may be added for a hotter curry. Preheat oven to moderate, 325°F.

Beat the egg whites until stiff but not dry. Fold into the lobster mixture carefully. Pour into a lightly buttered 1½-quart soufflé dish, and sprinkle the top with the almonds. Bake 35 minutes.

Serve at once.

Lobster Soufflé in the Shell

[4 servings]

6 tbsp. butter
⅜ cup sifted all-purpose flour
3 cups milk, scalded
2 boiled lobsters, split
6 egg yolks, beaten
1 tsp. salt
¼ tsp. pepper
¼ cup sliced, sautéed mushrooms
6 egg whites
2 tbsp. bread crumbs

Melt butter in a saucepan, add the flour, and stir until smooth. Add milk, stirring constantly. Cook 10 minutes, and set aside to cool.

Remove the meat from the lobsters, but reserve the shells. Grind or chop lobster meat coarsely, and add to the white sauce. Add the egg yolks slowly, beating steadily. Add salt, pepper, and mushrooms. Return to the heat, and cook 5 minutes, stirring almost constantly, but do not let boil. Set aside to cool for 10 minutes. Preheat oven to moderate, 350°F.

Beat the egg whites until stiff but not dry. Fold into the lobster mixture carefully. Place the lobster shells on a greased pan, and fill each shell about two-thirds full. Sprinkle bread crumbs on top. Bake 20 minutes.

Serve at once.

Oyster Soufflé

[4 servings]

¼ cup milk
¼ cup heavy cream
1 tsp. salt
⅛ tsp. pepper
½ cup instant tapioca
3 egg yolks, beaten
1 tbsp. butter, melted and cooled
¾ cup ground uncooked oysters (canned or fresh), drained
3 egg whites
dash cayenne pepper
2 tbsp. bread crumbs

Combine the milk, cream, salt, pepper, and tapioca in a saucepan, bring to a boil, stirring occasionally. Cook for 5 minutes over low heat, stirring constantly. Remove from heat, and let cool 10 minutes. Add the egg yolks gradually, stirring constantly. Add the butter, and stir; add oysters, and mix together thoroughly. Preheat oven to moderate, 350°F.

Beat the egg whites until stiff but not dry. Fold them into the oyster mixture carefully. Pour into an unbuttered 1½-quart soufflé dish, sprinkle cayenne pepper and bread crumbs over the top. Bake 25 minutes.

Serve at once.

Fresh-Salmon Soufflé

[4 servings]

½ cup white wine
¼ cup water
1 pound fresh salmon steak
1 bay leaf
2 whole peppercorns
1 tsp. salt

Combine wine and water in a shallow saucepan; add salmon, bay leaf, peppercorns, and salt. Cover and cook over low heat 20 minutes. Drain, reserving ¼ cup of the liquid. Let the fish cool for 20 minutes, then bone and flake it. Set aside. Now prepare:

3 tbsp. butter
2 tbsp. sifted all-purpose flour
¾ cup light cream, scalded
¼ cup reserved fish stock
½ tsp. salt
¼ tsp. pepper
6 egg whites
2 slices cooked bacon

Melt butter in a saucepan, add flour, and stir together well. Add cream, ¼ cup fish stock, salt, and pepper, stirring constantly. Cook 5 minutes, stirring occasionally. Add the salmon, and set aside to cool for 15 minutes. Preheat oven to moderate, 325°F.

Beat the egg whites until stiff but not dry. Fold them into the fish mixture carefully. Pour into a buttered, 1½-quart soufflé dish. Crumble the bacon on top. Bake 45 minutes.

Serve at once.

Two-Layer Salmon Soufflé

[4 servings]

2 tbsp. cornstarch
¾ cup milk
2 tbsp. butter
1 tsp. salt
¼ tsp. pepper
2 tsp. Worcestershire sauce
4 egg yolks, beaten
1 (7¾-oz.) can salmon
1 tsp. grated onion
1 cup ground cooked spinach
4 egg whites

Combine cornstarch in the top of a double boiler with 2 tablespoons of the milk, and stir to a smooth paste. Add the remaining milk, and place over boiling water. Cook and stir until the mixture boils. Cook until thick and smooth, about 5 minutes, stirring occasionally. Add the butter, salt, pepper, and Worcestershire, and mix well. Let cool for 5 minutes. Add the egg yolks gradually, mixing well. Set aside to cool again for 5 minutes.

Drain the salmon and flake it, adding the onion. Add half of the milk mixture to it, and stir well.

To the remaining half of the milk mixture, add the spinach, and mix well. Preheat oven to moderate, 350°F.

Beat the egg whites until stiff but not dry. Fold half of them into the spinach mixture carefully. Fold the other half of the whites into the salmon mixture carefully. Pour the spinach soufflé into a buttered 1½-quart soufflé dish. Spoon the salmon mixture on top gently. Bake 40 minutes.

Serve at once.

Shrimp-Jambalaya Soufflé

[4 servings]

3 tbsp. butter
3 tbsp. sifted all-purpose flour
1¼ cups canned tomato sauce
3 tbsp. chopped green pepper
3 tbsp. finely chopped onion
1 tsp. capers
4 egg yolks, beaten
1 cup coarsely chopped, cleaned, cooked shrimp
4 egg whites
¾ cup cooked rice
1 tsp. salt

Melt butter in a saucepan, add flour, and stir until smooth. Gradually add tomato sauce, stirring constantly until the boiling point is reached. Add green pepper, onion, and capers, and mix well. Cook 5 minutes, stirring occasionally. Let cool for 5 minutes.

Add the tomato mixture gradually to the beaten egg yolks in a bowl, stirring constantly. Add shrimp, and stir. Correct the seasoning. Set aside to cool for 5 minutes. Preheat oven to moderate, 350°F. Butter a 2-quart soufflé dish. Mix the rice with the salt, and spread it evenly in the bottom of the dish.

Beat the egg whites until stiff but not dry. Fold them into the shrimp mixture carefully. Pour the soufflé mixture on top of the rice. Place dish in a shallow pan of hot water. Bake 35 minutes.

Serve at once.

Shrimp-Mustard Soufflé

[4 servings]

- ¾ pound uncooked shrimp
- 1½ cups water
- 1 tsp. salt
- ¼ tsp. mixed pickling spice
- 1 onion, peeled and sliced
- 3 tbsp. butter
- 2 tbsp. sifted all-purpose flour
- ½ cup dry white wine
- ¼ cup heavy cream
- ¼ tsp. pepper
- 1 tbsp. lemon juice
- ½ tsp. dry mustard
- 4 egg yolks, beaten
- 4 egg whites

Place shrimp in saucepan with water, salt, pickling spice, and onion. Bring to a boil, and simmer 5 minutes. Drain, and reserve ½ cup stock. Remove the shells and veins from shrimp, and chop shrimp coarsely.

Melt butter in a saucepan, add flour, stirring until smooth. Combine the shrimp stock, wine, and cream, and gradually add to the flour mixture, stirring constantly. Bring to a boil, and cook 5 minutes, stirring occasionally. Add pepper, lemon juice, and mustard. Mix well, and let cool. Add the egg yolks, beating well. Add the shrimp, reserving a few pieces. Correct seasoning. Preheat oven to moderate, 350°F.

Beat the egg whites until stiff but not dry. Fold into shrimp mixture carefully. Pour into a buttered 1½-quart soufflé dish, and garnish with the remaining shrimp. Bake 35 minutes.

Serve at once.

Curried Shrimp-and-Pea Soufflé

[4 servings]

1 cup milk
1 tsp. corn syrup
¼ cup dried or grated fresh coconut
4 tbsp. butter
2 tbsp. grated onion
1 clove garlic, crushed
1 tbsp. curry powder
¼ tsp. powdered ginger
3 tbsp. sifted all-purpose flour
2 tbsp. cream
4 egg yolks, beaten
1 cup cooked peas
1 cup cooked shrimp, cleaned and chopped
½ tsp. salt
4 egg whites

Combine the milk, corn syrup, and coconut in a saucepan. Heat to the boiling point and stir. Set aside to cool for at least 20 minutes.

Melt the butter in another pan, add onion and garlic, and sauté 3 minutes. Add the curry powder and ginger. Beat in the cooled milk-and-coconut mixture, and cook 10 minutes, stirring occasionally.

Mix the flour and cream together in a bowl. Pour ½ cup of the hot milk mixture into it, mixing well, then return to the rest of the hot mixture and cook 3 minutes, stirring constantly. Slowly add to the egg yolks, stirring steadily to prevent curdling. Add peas, shrimp, and salt. Correct seasoning; if you like hot curries, a slight additional amount may be added. Preheat oven to moderate, 350°F.

Beat the egg whites until stiff but not dry. Fold into the shrimp mixture carefully. Pour into a buttered 1½-quart soufflé dish. Bake 30 minutes.

Serve at once.

Shrimp Soufflé in Green Peppers

[4 to 8 servings]

8 large green peppers
5 tbsp. butter
2 tbsp. grated onion
2 tbsp. sifted all-purpose flour
¾ cup milk, scalded
3 egg yolks
1 tsp. salt
¼ tsp. pepper
1 tbsp. chopped parsley
1 tsp. finely chopped chives
dash cayenne
1 cup ground cooked shrimp
3 tbsp. brandy
4 egg whites

Cut the stem from each pepper, being careful not to cut into the pepper. Slice off opposite end and remove seeds. Parboil 5 minutes, and drain. Brush the inside and outside of the peppers with a little melted butter. Set aside.

Sauté the onion in remaining butter 2 minutes, sprinkle with flour, stirring constantly; and continue cooking 5 minutes, stirring occasionally. Slowly add the milk, and continue stirring and cooking for 5 minutes longer. Set aside to cool 2 minutes.

Beat the egg yolks until light in color, and gradually add to the white sauce, beating constantly. Add the salt, pepper, parsley, chives, and cayenne, and stir. Return to the heat and bring to boiling point, stirring constantly. Lower the heat and simmer 3 minutes, stirring occasionally. Set aside to cool 5 minutes. Add the shrimp and the brandy; stir. Correct seasoning, and let cool 5 more minutes. Preheat oven to moderate, 325°F.

Beat the egg whites until stiff but not dry. Fold them into the shrimp mixture carefully.

Grease a baking sheet, and place the peppers on it. Fill each about two-thirds full of the soufflé mixture. Bake 30 minutes.

Serve at once.

Fillet-of-Sole Soufflé

[4 servings]

5 tbsp. butter
2 onions, peeled and chopped
2 carrots, scraped and chopped
3 sprigs parsley, chopped
4 fillets of sole
1 cup white wine
½ tsp. salt
¼ tsp. pepper
2 egg yolks
½ cup light cream

Melt the butter in a saucepan, add onions, carrots, and parsley; sauté over low heat 5 minutes, stirring frequently. Place the fish on top of the vegetables, and add the wine, salt, and pepper. Cover the pan, and let simmer 15 minutes. Remove the fillets carefully; strain sauce and discard the vegetables. Let sauce cool 10 minutes. Place the fillets in the bottom of a 2-quart buttered soufflé dish.

Beat the egg yolks in a saucepan until light in color, add cream and continue beating for 2 minutes longer. Slowly add the cooled fish sauce to the yolks and cream, beating constantly. Cook this mixture 5 minutes over low heat, but do not let boil. Stir constantly. Remove from heat and pour half over the fillets in the soufflé dish. Reserve the other half of this fish sauce. Now prepare:

2 tbsp. butter
2 tbsp. sifted all-purpose flour
1 cup stock, *or* 1 cup water and 1 chicken bouillon cube
½ tsp. salt
¼ tsp. pepper
3 egg yolks, beaten
4 egg whites

Melt the butter in a saucepan, add flour, and stir until smooth. Add stock gradually, beating constantly. Cook over low heat about 10 minutes, stirring occasionally, until sauce is reduced to about ¾ cup. Add salt and pepper, and stir. Remove from heat.

Beat the egg yolks until light in color; gradually add the stock sauce, beating constantly. Let cool for 10 minutes. Preheat oven to moderate, 375°F.

Beat the egg whites until stiff but not dry. Fold them into the yolk sauce carefully. Pour over the fillets in the soufflé dish. Bake 30 minutes.

Serve with the balance of the reheated fish sauce, previously reserved.

Serve at once.

Tuna-and-Cheese Soufflé

[4 servings]

- 4 tbsp. butter
- ¼ cup sifted all-purpose flour
- 1 cup milk, scalded
- ½ cup grated American *or* cheddar cheese
- 4 egg yolks, beaten
- 1 tsp. salt
- ½ tsp. pepper
- ¼ tsp. paprika
- 1 (7¾-oz.) can tuna fish
- ½ cup sliced mushrooms, sautéed
- 2 tbsp. sherry
- 4 egg whites

Melt the butter in a saucepan, add flour, and stir until smooth; add the milk, stirring constantly. Place over low heat and cook until thick, about 5 minutes, stirring occasionally. Add cheese and mix well. Add the egg yolks gradually, stirring constantly. Add salt, pepper, and paprika. Set aside to cool for 10 minutes.

Drain and flake the tuna fish. Combine with mushrooms and sherry, add to the cheese sauce, and mix both together well. Preheat oven to moderate, 350°F.

Beat the egg whites until stiff but not dry. Fold the whites into the fish mixture carefully.

Pour into an unbuttered 1½-quart soufflé dish. Bake 30 minutes.

Serve at once.

THREE

Cheese Soufflés

Cheese soufflés are often served as luncheon dishes, and also for light suppers. For those occasions they are ideal, especially when accompanied by a tossed green salad.

A cheese soufflé may also be served as an appetizer before a light main course. It is also good as an accompaniment to fish, meat, or green vegetables, in place of potatoes.

Although you may have made cheese soufflés before, you will find some unusual ones in this section, many of which have interesting textures and flavors.

The recipes supply enough for four to six people, when served as a side dish; but if the soufflé is the main dish of the meal there is enough for only two or three.

Brandied-Cheese Soufflé

[4 servings]

- 2 tbsp. butter
- ½ onion, peeled and grated
- 2 tbsp. sifted all-purpose flour
- 1½ cups stock, *or* 1½ cups water with 2 chicken bouillon cubes
- ¼ cup grated American cheese
- ¼ cup grated Parmesan cheese
- ⅛ tsp. salt
- dash cayenne pepper
- 3 egg yolks, beaten
- 3 egg whites
- 2 tbsp. brandy

Melt the butter in a saucepan, add onion, and sauté for 3 minutes. Add the flour, and stir until very smooth; add stock slowly, mixing constantly. Cook over low heat 10 minutes longer, or until the mixture is reduced to 1 cup.

Strain the sauce, return to very low heat and add the American cheese, and all but 1 tablespoon of the Parmesan cheese. Add the salt and cayenne pepper, and stir well. Add the egg yolks gradually, stirring constantly. Set aside to cool for 10 minutes. Preheat oven to moderate, 375°F.

Beat the egg whites until stiff but not dry. Fold them into the cheese mixture carefully. Pour into a buttered 1½-quart soufflé dish. Sprinkle the reserved tablespoon of Parmesan cheese on top. Bake 35 minutes.

Warm the 2 tablespoons of brandy, and set it aflame. Pour over the soufflé immediately before serving.

Serve at once.

Cheddar-Cheese Soufflé

[4 servings]

2 tbsp. butter
2 tbsp. sifted all-purpose flour
½ cup milk, scalded
1 tsp. salt
½ tsp. dry mustard
dash cayenne pepper
3 egg yolks, beaten
1 cup grated Cheddar cheese
3 egg whites
6 or 8 thin strips of cheddar cheese

Melt the butter in a saucepan, add the flour, and stir until smooth. Add the milk slowly, stirring constantly. Cook until thick and smooth, about 5 minutes, and then remove from the heat. Add salt, mustard, cayenne, and the beaten egg yolks, mixing steadily. Add the grated cheese, and return to low heat. Cook, stirring constantly, until cheese is completely melted. Set aside to cool for 15 minutes. Preheat oven to moderate, 375°F.

Beat the egg whites until stiff but not dry. Fold them into the cheese mixture carefully. Pour into a buttered 1½-quart soufflé dish, dusted with flour. Decorate the top with thin strips of cheese. Bake 35 minutes.

Serve at once.

Cheese Luncheon Soufflé

[4 servings]

8 slices bacon
2 tomatoes, halved
4 slices toast
2 tbsp. butter
2 tbsp. sifted all-purpose flour
½ cup milk, scalded
½ cup grated cheddar cheese
2 egg yolks, beaten
½ tsp. salt
dash cayenne
2 egg whites

Cook the bacon, but do not let it get crisp. Sauté the tomatoes in a little of the bacon fat, about 5 minutes.

Butter four 1½-cup soufflé dishes, and place a slice of toast on the bottom of each one. Place a tomato half on each piece of toast, and 2 slices of bacon over each piece of tomato.

Melt the butter in a saucepan, add flour, and stir until smooth. Add milk gradually, stirring constantly. Add cheese, and let melt, stirring occasionally. Let sauce cool for 5 minutes. Add the egg yolks, salt, and cayenne. Mix well, and let cool for 15 minutes. Preheat oven to moderate, 375°F.

Beat the egg whites until stiff but not dry. Fold them into the cheese mixture carefully. Pour into the soufflé dishes. Bake 20 minutes.

Serve at once.

Cheese-and-Farina Soufflé

[4 servings]

3 cups milk
¾ cup farina
4 tbsp. butter
1 tsp. salt
⅛ tsp. pepper
¾ cup grated Swiss cheese
4 egg yolks, beaten
4 egg whites

Heat the milk in a saucepan to boiling point, add the farina gradually, stirring constantly. Add butter, salt, and pepper, and continue cooking 20 minutes, stirring frequently. (It is important that there be no lumps in the farina.) Add all but 2 tablespoons of the cheese, and stir well. Remove from the heat and let cool for 10 minutes.

Beat the egg yolks until light in color; gradually add the cheese mixture to the yolks, beating constantly to prevent curdling. Let cool for 5 more minutes. Preheat oven to moderate, 350°F.

Beat the egg whites until stiff but not dry. Fold them into the cheese mixture carefully. Pour into an unbuttered 1½-quart soufflé dish, and sprinkle the remaining 2 tablespoons grated cheese on top. Place the soufflé dish in a shallow pan of hot water. Bake 30 minutes.

Serve at once.

Serve with Tomato Sauce, see page 223.

Cheese-Tapioca Soufflé

[4 servings]

1 cup milk
3 tbsp. quick-cooking tapioca
1 cup grated American *or* Gruyère cheese
dash cayenne pepper
½ tsp. dry mustard
1 tsp. salt
3 egg yolks, beaten
3 egg whites

Scald the milk in the top of a double boiler. Add tapioca, and cook over boiling water 15 minutes, stirring occasionally. Add cheese, stirring until melted. Then add cayenne, mustard, and salt, and mix. Let cool for 10 minutes.

Add the egg yolks gradually, beating well. Preheat oven to moderate, 350°F.

Beat the egg whites until stiff but not dry. Fold them into the cheese mixture carefully.

Pour into a buttered 1½-quart soufflé dish. Bake 25 minutes.

Serve at once.

Cheese-and-Toast Soufflé

[4 servings]

4 egg yolks
1½ cups light cream
1½ cups grated Swiss cheese
⅛ tsp. salt
dash cayenne pepper
dash grated nutmeg
4 slices toast, crusts trimmed
4 egg whites

Beat the egg yolks until light in color, and add cream. Beat well together. Add cheese, salt, cayenne, and nutmeg. Beat well. Preheat oven to moderate, 350°F.

Butter a 1½-quart soufflé dish thoroughly. Fit the slices of toast into the bottom of the dish.

Beat the egg whites until stiff but not dry. Fold them into the cheese mixture carefully. Pour the soufflé mixture into the dish. Place the dish in a shallow pan of hot water. Bake 30 minutes.

Serve at once.

Double-Boiler Parmesan Soufflé

[4 servings]

- 4 egg yolks
- ½ cup thick sour cream
- ¼ cup sifted all-purpose flour
- ¼ cup grated Parmesan cheese
- ½ tsp. salt
- ¼ tsp. pepper
- 4 egg whites
- 2 tbsp. bread crumbs
- 2 tbsp. Parmesan cheese for topping

Beat the egg yolks well; add sour cream, and continue beating until very smooth. In another bowl, mix flour, cheese, salt, and pepper. Gradually add the egg-and-sour-cream mixture to the flour mixture, stirring steadily.

Beat the egg whites until stiff but not dry. Fold them into the cream-and-flour mixture carefully.

Butter the top part of a 2-quart double boiler thoroughly. Sprinkle the bread crumbs evenly into it on the sides and bottom. Pour the soufflé mixture in. Place over hot water, and *cover*. Cook 50 minutes.

When ready, run a knife around the edge of the soufflé and unmold with care onto a warmed serving plate. Sprinkle Parmesan cheese on top.

Serve at once.

Individual Cheese Soufflés

[4 servings]

- ¾ cup milk
- 1½ cups soft bread crumbs
- 4 egg yolks
- ¾ cup grated American cheese
- 2 tbsp. butter, melted
- 4 egg whites

Scald the milk, add the bread crumbs, and mix well. Remove from the heat, and let cool for 5 minutes.

Beat the egg yolks in a bowl until light in color. Gradually add the milk mixture to the yolks, beating constantly to prevent curdling. Add the cheese and melted butter, and beat well. Let cool for 10 minutes more. Correct seasoning. Preheat oven to moderate, 350°F.

Beat the egg whites until stiff but not dry. Fold them into the cheese mixture carefully. Pour into four buttered 1½-cup soufflé dishes. Place the dishes in a shallow pan of hot water. Bake 20 minutes.

Serve at once.

Cheese soufflés are often served with green salads. A spicy French dressing used on the salad highlights the cheese flavor.

Macaroni-and-Cheese Soufflé

[4 servings]

3 tbsp. butter
2 tbsp. chopped onion
3 tbsp. sifted all-purpose flour
1 cup milk, scalded
1 tsp. salt
½ tsp. pepper
dash cayenne pepper
2 tbsp. chopped pimiento
4 egg yolks
¼ cup grated Cheddar cheese
¼ cup sliced mushrooms, sauteéd
1⅓ cups broken cooked macaroni
4 egg whites
2 tbsp. bread crumbs

Melt the butter in a saucepan, add onion, and sauté 2 minutes. Add flour, and stir until smooth. Add milk gradually, stirring constantly until boiling point is reached. Cook until thick and smooth over low heat, about 5 minutes, stirring occasionally. Add salt, pepper, cayenne, and pimiento, and mix well. Remove from heat, and let cool for 5 minutes.

Beat the egg yolks in a bowl until light in color. Gradually add the milk mixture to the yolks, stirring constantly. Add cheese, mushrooms, and macaroni, and mix again. Correct seasoning. Let cool for 5 minutes. Preheat oven to moderate, 350°F.

Beat the egg whites until stiff but not dry. Fold them into the cheese mixture carefully. Pour into a buttered 1½-quart soufflé dish, which has been dusted with the bread crumbs. Bake 35 minutes.

Serve at once.

Mushroom-and-Cheese Soufflé

[4 servings]

3 tbsp. butter
2 tbsp. sifted all-purpose flour
1 (11-oz.) can condensed mushroom soup
½ cup light cream
⅓ cup grated Cheddar cheese
½ tsp. salt
3 egg yolks, beaten
3 egg whites

Melt the butter in a saucepan, add flour, stirring until smooth. Add the soup and cream, and mix well. Add the cheese, and cook over low heat 3 minutes, stirring until cheese melts. Let cool for 5 minutes.

Add salt and the egg yolks; remove from the heat and let cool for 15 minutes. Preheat oven to moderate, 350°F.

Beat the egg whites until stiff but not dry. Fold them into the cheese mixture carefully. Pour into a buttered 1½-quart soufflé dish. Bake 30 minutes.

Serve at once.

Sour-Cream Soufflé

[4 servings]

1½ cups thick sour cream	5 egg yolks
1 cup sifted all-purpose flour	5 egg whites
1 tsp. salt	4 tbsp. butter, melted
½ tsp. pepper	4 tbsp. grated Parmesan cheese

Beat the sour cream, flour, salt, and pepper together until smooth, about 5 minutes. Beat the egg yolks until light in color. Gradually add to the sour cream mixture, beating constantly. Preheat oven to moderate, 350°F.

Beat the egg whites until stiff but not dry. Fold them into the cream mixture carefully. Pour into a buttered 1½-quart soufflé dish. Place in a shallow pan of hot water. Bake 35 minutes.

Serve at once.

Serve with the melted butter, and sprinkled with Parmesan cheese. This soufflé is especially good served with roast beef, in place of potatoes.

Spicy-Cheese Soufflé

[4 servings]

½ cup tomato juice
1 tsp. Worcestershire sauce
½ tsp. salt
1 bay leaf
6 tbsp. butter
3 tbsp. sifted all-purpose flour
1 cup grated Cheddar cheese
½ tsp. dry mustard
4 egg yolks, beaten
1 tbsp. brandy
4 egg whites

In an enamel or glass saucepan, combine the tomato juice with the Worcestershire sauce, salt, and bay leaf. Bring to boiling, lower the heat, and cook 10 minutes longer. Strain.

Melt the butter in another saucepan, add flour, and mix well. Add tomato juice mixture, stirring steadily. Cook until thick and smooth, about 5 minutes, stirring occasionally. Add cheese and mustard, stirring together well. Let cool for 15 minutes. Add beaten egg yolks and brandy, and stir thoroughly. Preheat oven to moderate, 325°F.

Beat the egg whites until stiff but not dry. Fold them into the cheese mixture carefully. Pour into an unbuttered 1½-quart soufflé dish. Bake 35 minutes.

Serve at once.

This soufflé is often served with a mixed green salad.

Baked-Tomatoes-with-Cheese Soufflé

[4 to 8 servings]

- 8 large firm tomatoes
- ¼ cup heavy cream
- 2 tbsp. sifted all-purpose flour
- 2 tbsp. butter, melted
- 4 egg yolks, beaten
- ½ tsp. salt
- ¼ tsp. pepper
- ¾ cup grated Swiss *or* Parmesan cheese
- 4 egg whites

Cut a 1-inch slice off the top of each tomato. Remove the pulp carefully, and turn tomatoes upside down to drain.

Combine cream and flour in a saucepan and mix until smooth. Add butter, egg yolks, salt, and pepper, and stir. Cook over low heat until thick, stirring constantly, about 5 minutes. Add the cheese, and stir until cheese melts. Let cool for 15 minutes. Preheat oven to moderate, 350°F.

Beat the egg whites until stiff but not dry. Fold them into the cheese mixture carefully. Spoon the mixture into the tomatoes until they are about three-quarters full. Place on a greased baking sheet. Bake 25 minutes.

Serve at once.

FOUR

Poultry Soufflés

No one ever knows what to do with leftover turkey, and of course there's always a little cooked chicken that never is used. Instead of serving these leftovers as cold meats, or hash, a poultry soufflé may surprise and please your family. It's truly a delightful way of utilizing leftover poultry.

Poultry soufflés are good for luncheon dishes, and will be greatly admired. They are excellent Sunday-night supper dishes, too.

For an unusual and also a more substantial dish, individual soufflé dishes may be lined with a pastry crust. Prebake the pastry crust in a moderate oven, 350°F., 15 minutes. Remove and cool for 30 minutes before adding soufflé mixture; then proceed as directed in the individual soufflé recipe.

Chicken-Curry Soufflé

[4 servings]

3 tbsp. olive oil
1 onion, peeled and chopped
3 tbsp. sifted all-purpose flour
1¼ cups milk, scalded
1 tbsp. curry powder
½ tsp. salt
1 green pepper, finely chopped
2 tbsp. finely chopped pimiento
3 egg yolks, beaten
½ cup cooked rice
1 cup chopped cooked chicken
4 egg whites

Heat the olive oil in a saucepan, add the onion and sauté until brown, stirring occasionally. Sprinkle with flour and stir until smooth. Gradually add the milk, stirring constantly until boiling point is reached. Add the curry, salt, green pepper, and pimiento, and cook over low heat 10 minutes longer, stirring occasionally. Set aside to cool for 10 minutes. Add the egg yolks, stirring constantly. Add rice and chicken, and mix well. Correct seasoning. Preheat oven to moderate, 350°F.

Beat the egg whites until stiff but not dry. Fold them into the chicken mixture carefully. Pour into an unbuttered 1½-quart soufflé dish. Bake 35 minutes.

Serve at once.

Orleans Chicken Soufflé

[4 to 8 servings]

8 medium tomatoes
3 tbsp. butter
2 tbsp. grated onion
3 tbsp. sifted all-purpose flour
¾ cup light cream, scalded
3 egg yolks
1 tsp. salt
¼ tsp. pepper
dash cayenne pepper
2 tsp. chopped parsley
1 tbsp. brandy
1 cup finely chopped cooked chicken
3 egg whites

Cut 1-inch slice off the stem end of each tomato. Scoop out the seeds and pulp, leaving a thick shell. Turn upside down and drain.

Melt butter in a saucepan, add onion and sauté 2 minutes, stirring well. Add flour, and stir until smooth. Gradually add the cream, stirring constantly until boiling point is reached. Beat the egg yolks in a bowl. Pour a few tablespoons of the hot mixture gradually into the egg yolks, beating steadily; then pour this back into the hot mixture, stirring constantly. Cook over low heat until thick and smooth, about 5 minutes, stirring frequently. Add salt, pepper, cayenne, parsley, brandy, and chicken, and mix well. Remove from heat and let cool for 10 minutes. Preheat oven to moderate, 375°F.

Beat the egg whites until stiff but not dry. Fold them into the chicken mixture carefully. Spoon the mixture into the tomato shells about three-quarters full. Place on a greased baking sheet. Bake 20 minutes.

Serve at once.

Portugaise Chicken Soufflé

[4 servings]

- 3 tbsp. butter
- 2 tbsp. chopped onion
- 3 tbsp. sifted all-purpose flour
- ½ cup red wine
- ½ cup canned tomato sauce
- ½ cup stock, *or* ½ cup water and 1 chicken bouillon cube
- ½ tsp. salt
- ¼ tsp. pepper
- 2 tbsp. chopped parsley
- 1 tomato, peeled and chopped
- 3 egg yolks, beaten
- 1 cup coarsely chopped cooked chicken
- 3 egg whites

Melt the butter in a saucepan, add onion and sauté 2 minutes. Add the flour, stirring constantly until smooth. Combine wine, tomato sauce, and stock, and add very slowly to the flour mixture, stirring constantly until the boiling point is reached. Add the salt, pepper, parsley, and tomato. Cook over low heat 10 minutes, stirring occasionally. Let cool for 10 minutes. Add the egg yolks, beating well. Add chicken; correct seasoning, and mix well. Preheat oven to moderate, 375°F.

Beat the egg whites until stiff but not dry. Fold them into the chicken mixture carefully. Pour into a 1½-quart unbuttered soufflé dish. Bake 30 minutes.

Serve at once.

Duck Soufflé

[4 servings]

- 3 tbsp. butter
- 3 tbsp. sifted all-purpose flour
- 1 cup light cream, scalded
- 1 cup stock, *or* 1 cup water and 1 chicken bouillon cube
- 1 tsp. salt
- ½ tsp. pepper
- 2 tbsp. grated onion
- 2 tbsp. chopped parsley
- 3 tbsp. sherry
- 1 tbsp. chopped pimiento
- 1½ cups finely chopped cooked duck
- 3 egg yolks, beaten
- 3 egg whites
- 2 tbsp. bread crumbs

Melt butter in a saucepan, add the flour, stirring steadily. Add cream and stock gradually, stirring constantly; cook the mixture 5 minutes. Add salt, pepper, onion, parsley, sherry, pimiento, and duck. Beat well. Cool 10 minutes. Add the egg yolks, and again mix well. Preheat oven to moderate, 350°F.

Beat the egg whites until stiff but not dry. Fold them into the duck mixture carefully. Pour into buttered 1½-quart soufflé dish, dusted with bread crumbs. Bake 35 minutes.

Serve at once.

Duck Soufflé, Escoffier

[4 servings]

4 egg yolks
2 tbsp. sherry
1 cup hot stock, *or* 1 cup water and 1 chicken bouillon cube
1 cup finely chopped cooked duck
4 sautéed chicken livers, chopped
1½ tsp. salt
¾ tsp. pepper
dash cayenne pepper
1 tsp. chopped parsley
1 tbsp. chopped onion
4 egg whites

Beat the egg yolks in a bowl, add the sherry and continue beating until the mixture is frothy. Gradually add the hot stock, beating steadily. Add the duck meat, chicken livers, salt, pepper, cayenne, parsley, and onion, and stir well. Set aside to cool for 10 minutes. Preheat oven to moderate, 375°F.

Beat the egg whites until stiff but not dry. Fold them into the duck mixture carefully. Pour into an unbuttered 1½-quart soufflé dish, and place in a shallow pan of hot water. Bake 30 minutes.

Serve at once.

This soufflé may be served with a Tomato Vinaigrette Sauce, see page 220.

Flemish Duck Soufflé

[4 servings]

4 tbsp. butter
2 tbsp. chopped parsley
2 tbsp. chopped onion
2 tbsp. chopped green pepper
3 tbsp. sifted all-purpose flour
1 cup dry white wine
1 tsp. anchovy paste
½ cup finely chopped green olives
¼ tsp. salt
¼ tsp. pepper
3 egg yolks, beaten
1 cup chopped cooked duck
3 egg whites

Melt the butter in a saucepan, add parsley, onion, and green pepper, and stir together. Sauté 2 minutes. Sprinkle the flour on top, stirring until very smooth. Gradually add the wine, stirring constantly until the mixture is at the boiling point. Cook until thick and smooth, about 5 minutes, stirring occasionally. Add anchovy paste, olives, salt, and pepper, and mix. Set aside to cool for 5 minutes. Add the egg yolks gradually, stirring well. Add the duck, mix together. Correct seasoning, bearing in mind that this soufflé is somewhat spicy. Preheat oven to moderate 350°F.

Beat the egg whites until stiff but not dry. Fold them into the duck mixture carefully. Pour into an unbuttered 1½-quart soufflé dish. Bake 35 minutes.

Serve at once.

Game Soufflé

[4 servings]

- 2 cups ground cooked partridge, goose, or guinea hen
- 3 egg yolks, beaten
- ½ tsp. salt
- ¼ tsp. pepper
- 5 tbsp. butter
- 3 tbsp. sifted all-purpose flour
- 1 cup light cream, scalded
- 2 tsp. chopped parsley
- 2 tbsp. grated onion
- 1 tbsp. brandy
- 4 egg whites

Combine the game with egg yolks, salt, and pepper, and mix well. Chill in the refrigerator for at least 1 hour.

Melt the butter in a saucepan, add flour, and mix until smooth; add cream, cook, stirring constantly until thick and smooth, about 5 minutes. Add parsley, onion, and brandy, and stir. Let cool for 10 minutes. Combine with the game-and-egg mixture, and stir all together. Correct the seasoning. Preheat oven to moderate, 350°F.

Beat the egg whites until stiff but not dry. Fold them into the game mixture carefully. Pour into an unbuttered 1½-quart soufflé dish. Bake 40 minutes.

Serve at once.

Giblets-and-Liver Soufflé

[4 servings]

1 (10½-oz.) can condensed mushroom soup
1 cup finely chopped cooked chicken giblets, chicken livers, or both, half and half
½ tsp. salt
2 tbsp. white wine
3 egg yolks, beaten
3 egg whites

Heat soup in a saucepan, add the giblets (or chicken livers, or both), salt, and wine. Mix well, heat thoroughly and remove from the heat. Let cool for 10 minutes. Add the egg yolks slowly, beating steadily. Correct seasoning, adding ¼ tsp. pepper, if desired. Preheat oven to moderate, 350°F.

Beat the egg whites until stiff but not dry. Fold them into the giblet mixture carefully. Pour into an unbuttered 1½-quart soufflé dish. Bake 35 minutes.

Serve at once.

Smoked-Turkey Soufflé

[4 servings]

- 1 cup finely chopped smoked turkey
- 3 egg yolks
- ⅓ cup chopped mushrooms
- 1 tbsp. butter
- dash cayenne pepper
- ½ cup heavy cream
- 3 egg whites

The smoked turkey should be cut fine, but not ground. Beat the egg yolks until light in color; combine with the turkey. Set aside. Sauté the mushrooms in the butter; let cool for 5 minutes. Combine with the turkey mixture; add cayenne and stir. Whip cream, and fold into the turkey mixture. Preheat oven to moderate, 350°F.

Beat the egg whites until stiff but not dry. Fold into the turkey mixture carefully. Pour into four buttered 1½-cup soufflé dishes. Bake 20 minutes.

Serve at once.

Tetrazzini Soufflé

[4 servings]

- 2 tbsp. butter
- 3 tbsp. sifted all-purpose flour
- 1 cup light cream, scalded
- 1 onion, peeled and sliced
- 1 bay leaf
- 1 tsp. salt
- ½ tsp. pepper
- 4 egg yolks
- 1 cup cooked turkey *or* chicken, cut in thin julienne strips
- 1 cup sliced mushrooms, sautéed
- ½ cup chopped cooked spaghetti
- 4 egg whites
- 2 tbsp. bread crumbs
- 2 tbsp. grated Parmesan cheese

Melt the butter in a saucepan, add flour, and stir until smooth. Gradually add cream, stirring constantly until the boiling point is reached. Add onion, bay leaf, salt, and pepper, and mix well. Cook until thick and smooth, about 5 minutes, stirring occasionally. Discard bay leaf. Beat the egg yolks in a bowl until light in color, add the cream sauce to the yolks gradually, beating constantly. Add turkey or chicken, mushrooms, and spaghetti, and stir well. Correct seasoning. Let cool for 10 minutes. Preheat oven to moderate, 350°F.

Beat the egg whites until stiff but not dry. Fold them into the turkey or chicken mixture carefully. Pour into a buttered 2-quart soufflé dish dusted with bread crumbs. Sprinkle the top with Parmesan cheese. Bake 35 minutes.

Serve at once.

FIVE

Meat Soufflés

The soufflé is a glamorous way of using leftover meats. If a meat soufflé is to be the main dish of dinner, it will serve only about 2 portions. But as a secondary dish, there is sufficient in these recipes for 4 servings. In some cases, you may find that there is enough for 6 servings, especially when the soufflé is a rich mixture. Since no two people eat the same quantity of food, it is a matter of knowing your diners and their capacity.

Meat soufflés should be served with boiled or baked potatoes. Fried potatoes do not go well with soufflés.

Beef-Ring Soufflé

[4 servings]

½ cup butter
3 eggs
2 tbsp. sherry
¼ cup soft bread crumbs
1¼ pounds finely ground, uncooked beef
½ cup ground uncooked mushrooms (about ¼ pound)
½ tsp. pepper
1 tsp. salt
2 egg whites

Cream the butter in a bowl, add the eggs, beating until light. Add the sherry and bread crumbs and beat again. Combine beef, mushrooms, pepper, and salt. Mix thoroughly. Add to the crumb mixture and mix very well. Preheat oven to moderate, 325°F.

Beat the egg whites until stiff but not dry. Fold into the beef mixture carefully. Pour into a buttered 7-inch ring mold. Cover, and place in a shallow pan of hot water. Bake 1 hour.

Run a knife around the edge, tap gently on all sides, and turn onto a warmed plate, allowing the mold to remain in place for 2 minutes.

Serve at once.

Serve with Beef-Mushroom Sauce, see page 222.

Hamburger Soufflé

[4 servings]

- 2 tbsp. butter
- 2 tbsp. sifted all-purpose flour
- 1 cup light cream
- 2 tbsp. grated onion
- 2 tbsp. chopped parsley
- ¼ cup soft bread crumbs
- ½ pound ground uncooked beef
- 1 tsp. Worcestershire sauce
- 1 tsp. salt
- ½ tsp. pepper
- 4 egg yolks
- 5 egg whites

Melt the butter in a saucepan, add flour and stir until smooth. Add cream gradually, stirring constantly. Simmer 10 minutes, stirring occasionally. Add the onion, parsley, bread crumbs, beef, Worcestershire, salt, and pepper, and stir well. Remove from heat, and let cool for 10 minutes. Beat the egg yolks until light in color. Add them gradually to the beef mixture, beating constantly. Preheat oven to moderate, 375°F.

Beat the egg whites until stiff but not dry. Fold them into the beef mixture carefully. Pour into four buttered 1½-cup soufflé dishes. Bake 20 minutes.

Serve at once.

Serve with Tomato Sauce, see page 223.

Corned-Beef Soufflé

[4 servings]

- 3 tbsp. butter
- 3 tbsp. sifted all-purpose flour
- 1¼ cups milk, scalded
- ½ tsp. salt
- ¼ tsp. pepper
- 1 tbsp. olive oil
- 1 clove garlic, minced
- 2 onions, peeled and chopped
- 3 tbsp. chopped parsley
- ½ tsp. dry mustard
- 4 egg yolks, beaten
- 1¼ cups finely chopped cooked corned beef
- 4 egg whites

Melt the butter in a saucepan, add flour, and stir until smooth. Gradually add the milk, stirring continuously, until the boiling point is reached. Add salt and pepper, and continue cooking until thick and smooth, about 5 minutes, stirring occasionally. Set aside to cool for 5 minutes.

In another saucepan, heat the oil, garlic, onions, parsley, and mustard, and stir well. Cook 5 minutes over low heat, stirring occasionally. Set aside to cool for 5 minutes. Add the egg yolks gradually to the white sauce, beating constantly to prevent curdling. Add onion mixture, and corned beef, and mix all together thoroughly. Correct seasoning, and let cool for 10 minutes. Preheat oven to moderate, 350°F.

Beat the egg whites until stiff but not dry. Fold them into the beef mixture carefully. Pour into a buttered 1½-quart soufflé dish. Bake 30 minutes.

Serve at once.

Calves'-Brains Soufflé

[4 servings]

3 calves' brains
2 cups water
1 tbsp. vinegar

Wash the brains thoroughly in cold water. Drain. Cover with the water and vinegar, and bring to a boil; simmer 10 minutes. Drain, plunge into cold water. When cool, remove the membrane. Chop brains coarsely.

Now prepare:

2 tbsp. butter
1 tbsp. sifted all-purpose flour
1 cup light cream, scalded
1 tsp. salt
¼ tsp. pepper
1 tbsp. onion juice
2 egg yolks
3 egg whites

Melt the butter in a saucepan, add flour, and stir until smooth. Add cream very slowly, stirring constantly. Add salt and pepper, and continue cooking over low heat 5 minutes, stirring frequently. Add the chopped brains and onion juice, mix and remove from the heat. Let cool for 10 minutes. Beat the egg yolks until light in color; add to the brain mixture gradually, beating constantly. Correct the seasoning. Preheat oven to moderate, 325°F.

Beat the egg whites until stiff but not dry. Fold into the brain mixture carefully. Pour into four buttered 1½-cup soufflé dishes. Bake 20 minutes.

Serve at once.

Serve with Mushroom-Almond Sauce, see page 221.

Ham Soufflé

[4 servings]

- 2 tbsp. butter
- 2 tbsp. sifted all-purpose flour
- 1½ cups stock, *or* 1½ cups boiling water and 2 chicken bouillon cubes

Melt the butter in a saucepan, add flour, and stir until smooth. Add the stock gradually, stirring constantly. Cook over low heat 15 minutes, stirring frequently. Remove from heat. There should be about ¾ cup of sauce.

Now prepare:

- 1 tbsp. butter
- 1½ cups finely chopped cooked ham
- 4 egg yolks
- ½ tsp. salt
- ¼ tsp. pepper
- 5 egg whites

Melt the butter in a saucepan, heat the ham in it slowly; do not let the ham brown. Gradually add ¾ cup of the white sauce which had been set aside, stirring constantly. Remove from heat, and let cool for 10 minutes. Beat the egg yolks in a bowl until light in color. Add the ham mixture slowly to the yolks, beating constantly. Add salt and pepper, stir. Let cool for 5 more minutes. Preheat oven to moderate, 375°F.

Beat the egg whites until stiff but not dry. Fold them into the ham mixture carefully. Pour into an unbuttered 1½-quart soufflé dish. Bake 30 minutes.

Serve at once.

Ham Soufflé, Gastronome

[4 servings]

- 3 tbsp. butter
- 2 tbsp. sifted all-purpose flour
- 1¼ cups stock, *or* 1¼ cups boiling water and 1 chicken bouillon cube
- ¼ tsp. pepper
- 4 egg yolks
- ¼ cup minced mushrooms, sautéed
- 1 cup finely ground cooked ham
- ¾ cup fine noodles, cooked and drained
- 2 tbsp. butter, melted
- 4 egg whites

Melt the butter in a saucepan, add flour, and stir until smooth. Gradually add stock, stirring constantly until the boiling point is reached. Simmer 5 minutes, stirring occasionally. Add the pepper and stir. Beat the egg yolks in a bowl, and pour the hot mixture gradually into the yolks, beating constantly to prevent curdling. Add mushrooms and ham, and mix well. Correct the seasoning. Set aside to cool for 10 minutes. Preheat oven to hot, 400°F. Butter a 2-quart soufflé dish, and place the cooked noodles on the bottom. Pour the melted butter on the noodles.

Beat the egg whites until stiff but not dry. Fold them into the mushroom and ham mixture carefully. Pour the soufflé mixture on top of the noodles. Set in a shallow pan of hot water. Bake 35 minutes.

Serve at once.

Ham-and-Asparagus Soufflé

[4 servings]

3 tbsp. butter
1 onion, peeled and chopped
3 tbsp. sifted all-purpose flour
1 cup stock, *or* 1 cup water and 1 chicken bouillon cube
½ cup light cream
¼ tsp. pepper
1 cup ground cooked ham
4 egg yolks, beaten
4 egg whites
8 cooked asparagus tips

Melt the butter in a saucepan, add onion and sauté 2 minutes. Sprinkle flour on top, stir and cook 5 minutes. Gradually add stock and cream, stirring constantly until the boiling point is reached. Cook 5 minutes more, stirring occasionally. Add pepper, and mix; strain. There should be 1 cup of sauce. Let cool for 10 minutes. Add the ham and the egg yolks, beating steadily. Correct seasoning. Preheat oven to moderate, 350°F.

Beat the egg whites until stiff but not dry. Fold them into the ham mixture carefully. Pour half of the mixture into a buttered 1½-quart soufflé dish. Arrange the asparagus on top, and pour the remaining soufflé mixture over the asparagus. Bake 35 minutes.

Serve at once.

Ham Soufflé, Carmen

[4 servings]

3 tbsp. butter
3 tbsp. sifted all-purpose flour
1 cup canned tomato sauce
1/4 cup water
4 egg yolks
1 cup finely ground cooked ham
2 tbsp. chopped pimiento
4 egg whites
1 pimiento, cut in julienne strips

Melt butter in a saucepan, add flour, stirring constantly, until smooth. Add tomato sauce and water gradually, stirring constantly until the boiling point is reached. Cook until smooth and thick, about 5 minutes, stirring occasionally. Beat the egg yolks in a bowl. Pour the sauce gradually into the yolks, beating constantly. Add ham and pimiento. Correct the seasoning. Mix thoroughly. Let cool for 15 minutes. Preheat oven to hot, 400°F.

Beat the egg whites until stiff but not dry. Fold into the ham mixture carefully. Pour into a buttered 1½-quart soufflé dish. Arrange the pimiento strips on top. Place in a shallow pan of hot water. Bake 35 minutes.

Serve at once.

Ham-and-Spinach Soufflé

[4 servings]

2 tbsp. butter
1 cup chopped cooked spinach
1 tbsp. sifted all-purpose flour
1 tsp. salt
½ tsp. pepper
½ cup hot chicken stock, *or* ½ cup boiling water and 1 chicken bouillon cube
1 cup chopped cooked lean ham
5 tbsp. grated Gruyère cheese
3 egg yolks, beaten
4 egg whites

Melt the butter in a saucepan. Drain spinach, add to the butter, and cook slowly about 5 minutes. Sprinkle with the flour, salt, and pepper, and mix well. Add stock, stirring constantly. Bring to a boil, and cook covered 10 minutes. Stir; let cool for 15 minutes. Add the ham, cheese, and egg yolks gradually, mixing well. Preheat oven to moderate, 350°F.

Beat the egg whites until stiff but not dry. Fold them into the ham mixture carefully. Pour into an unbuttered 1½-quart soufflé dish. Bake 25 minutes.

Serve at once.

Prosciutto-Ham Soufflé

[4 servings]

- 5 egg yolks
- 1/4 tsp. salt
- 1/4 tsp. pepper
- 3 tbsp. grated Parmesan cheese
- 1/2 pound trimmed prosciutto ham, cut in thin julienne strips
- 1/2 cup melted butter, cooled
- 5 egg whites

Beat the egg yolks in a bowl, until light in color. Add salt, pepper, and cheese; beat well for 1 minute. Add the prosciutto ham and the melted butter, and stir well. Preheat oven to moderate, 350°F. Beat the egg whites until stiff but not dry. Fold into the ham mixture carefully. Pour into a buttered 1½-quart soufflé dish. Bake 25 minutes.

Serve at once.

This soufflé is delicious served with a tomato salad, or it may accompany a sweetbreads dish.

Ham-and-Egg Soufflé

[4 servings]

2 tbsp. butter
2 tbsp. sifted all-purpose flour
1 tsp. salt
½ tsp. pepper
dash cayenne pepper
1 tbsp. grated onion
1 cup white wine
1 tbsp. chopped parsley
3 egg yolks, beaten
2 cups ground cooked ham
1 cup bread crumbs
3 egg whites
4 eggs
1 tsp. paprika

Melt the butter in a saucepan, add flour, salt, pepper, cayenne, and onion. Stir until smooth. Add the wine, stirring constantly. Cook 5 minutes, and continue stirring. Add the parsley and egg yolks, beating well. Mix the ham and bread crumbs together, and add to the mixture. Correct the seasoning, and let cool for 15 minutes. Preheat oven to moderate, 350°F.

Beat the egg whites until stiff but not dry. Fold them into the ham mixture carefully. Pour into four buttered 1½-cup soufflé dishes. With a spoon, make a depression in the center of each, and carefully break a whole egg into it. Sprinkle the top with paprika. Bake 20 minutes.

Serve at once.

Lamb Soufflé

[4 servings]

4 tbsp. butter
2 tbsp. chopped onion
¼ cup sifted all-purpose flour
1 cup stock, *or* 1 cup boiling water and 1 chicken bouillon cube
½ cup light cream, scalded
½ tsp. salt
¼ tsp. dry mustard
2 slices lemon
4 egg yolks
1 tsp. wine vinegar
1 cup finely chopped cooked lamb
2 tbsp. capers, drained
4 egg whites

Melt the butter in a saucepan, add the onion, and sauté 2 minutes. Add flour, and stir until smooth. Add the stock and cream gradually, stirring steadily. Add salt, mustard, and lemon slices. Cook over low heat until thick and smooth, about 5 minutes, stirring constantly. Strain. Set aside to cool for 5 minutes. Beat the egg yolks in a bowl until light in color. Add the cream mixture gradually to the yolks, beating constantly to prevent curdling. Add vinegar, lamb, and capers, and mix thoroughly. Correct seasoning. Let cool 5 more minutes. Preheat oven to moderate, 350°F.

Beat the egg whites until stiff but not dry. Fold them into the lamb mixture carefully. Pour into a buttered 1½-quart soufflé dish. Bake 35 minutes. Serve with baked potatoes.

Serve at once.

Pork Soufflé

[4 servings]

2 tbsp. butter, melted
4 egg yolks, beaten
½ cup milk
1 onion, peeled and grated
1 clove garlic, minced
2 tbsp. chopped parsley
2 tbsp. chopped pimiento
1 tbsp. brandy
1 tsp. salt
½ tsp. pepper
dash cayenne pepper
1½ cups finely ground cooked lean pork
4 egg whites

Combine melted butter and egg yolks in a bowl and beat together. Add milk, onion, garlic, parsley, pimiento, brandy, salt, pepper, and cayenne. Beat all together vigorously for 1 minute. Add pork and mix well. Preheat oven to moderate, 375°F.

Beat the egg whites until stiff but not dry. Fold them into the pork mixture carefully. Pour into four buttered 1½-cup soufflé dishes. Bake 30 minutes.

Serve at once.

Sausage-and-Spinach Soufflé

[4 servings]

3 tbsp. butter
3 tbsp. sifted all-purpose flour
1 cup stock, *or* 1 cup boiling water and 1 chicken bouillon cube
1 cup chopped cooked spinach
½ tsp. salt
¼ tsp. pepper
3 egg yolks, beaten
5 small pork sausages
3 egg whites

Melt the butter in a saucepan, add flour, and stir until smooth. Add stock, stirring occasionally. Cook over low heat 5 minutes, stirring occasionally. Add spinach, salt, and pepper, and mix well. Add the egg yolks gradually, stirring constantly. Set aside to cool for 15 minutes.

Slice sausages into ½-inch pieces, and cook in a hot, ungreased frying pan until done, about 15 minutes; drain. Reserve 5 pieces of sausage, and add the rest to the spinach mixture, stirring well. Preheat oven to moderate, 350°F.

Beat the egg whites until stiff but not dry. Fold them into the sausage-spinach mixture carefully. Pour into a 1½-quart soufflé dish which has been lightly buttered. Place the reserved pieces of sausage on top to form a circle. Bake 35 minutes.

Serve at once.

Indian Luncheon Soufflé

[4 servings]

½ cup yellow corn meal
1 tsp. salt
½ cup cold milk
1½ cups hot milk
4 egg yolks
½ tsp. pepper
dash grated nutmeg
8 pork sausages
4 egg whites
4 whole eggs

Mix the corn meal, salt, and cold milk into a smooth paste. Gradually add this paste to hot milk, in the top part of a double boiler, stirring constantly. Place over hot water, and cook 30 minutes, stirring occasionally. Remove from heat. Beat the egg yolks in a bowl until light in color. Add the corn-meal mixture gradually, stirring constantly to prevent curdling. Add pepper and nutmeg, and stir. Correct the seasoning and set aside to cool for 10 minutes.

Fry sausages until brown, but not crisp. Drain, and set aside. Preheat oven to moderate, 350°F. Butter four 1½-cup soufflé dishes, and place 2 sausages in each.

Beat the egg whites until stiff but not dry. Fold them into the corn-meal mixture carefully. Pour soufflé mixture over the sausages.

Bake 20 minutes. Gently open the oven, make an indentation with a spoon on each soufflé and break an egg in each. Continue baking for 10 minutes more.

Serve at once.

Veal Soufflé

[4 servings]

1½ cups chopped cooked veal
¾ cup chopped mushrooms, sautéed
1 tbsp. minced onion
1½ tbsp. butter
½ tsp. salt
½ tsp. paprika
dash cayenne pepper
½ cup heavy cream, scalded
3 egg whites
¼ cup chopped blanched almonds

Place the veal in a saucepan, add mushrooms, onion, butter, salt, paprika, and cayenne. Mix well, add cream and stir over moderate heat until very smooth, about 3 minutes. Preheat oven to moderate, 350°F.

Beat the egg whites until stiff but not dry. Fold them carefully into the veal mixture. Pour into four buttered 1½-cup soufflé dishes which have been sprinkled with about half of the chopped almonds. Sprinkle the rest of the almonds on top. Bake 20 minutes.

Serve at once.

Liver-and-Bacon Soufflé

[4 servings]

- ½ pound liver, uncooked
- 1 onion, peeled
- 1 bay leaf
- 1 clove garlic
- 1 cup water

Combine the liver, onion, bay leaf, garlic, and water in a saucepan and bring to a boil, and simmer gently for 10 minutes. Drain, remove any membranes from the liver; grind liver fine in a food mill. Set aside.

Now prepare:

- 3 tbsp. butter
- 1 tbsp. finely chopped onion
- 3 tbsp. sifted all-purpose flour
- 1 cup light cream, scalded
- 1 tsp. salt
- ¼ tsp. pepper
- 1 tbsp. chopped parsley
- 4 egg yolks
- 4 strips crisp bacon, crumbled
- 4 egg whites

Melt the butter in a saucepan, add onion, and sauté 2 minutes. Add flour, and stir until smooth. Add cream gradually, stirring constantly, until the mixture boils. Cook until thick and smooth, about 5 minutes, stirring occasionally. Add salt, pepper, and parsley, and mix. Beat the egg yolks in a bowl until light in color. Add the hot mixture slowly to the yolks, stirring constantly to prevent curdling. Add the ground liver and bacon and mix all together well. Correct the seasoning. Let cool for 10 minutes. Preheat oven to moderate, 375°F.

Beat the egg whites until stiff but not dry. Fold them into the liver mixture carefully. Pour into a buttered 1½-quart soufflé dish. Bake 30 minutes.

Serve at once.

Sweetbreads Soufflé

[4 servings]

- 1 pair calf's sweetbreads
- 1 tbsp. vinegar
- 2 tbsp. butter
- 3 tbsp. sifted all-purpose flour
- 1 cup light cream, scalded
- 1 tsp. salt
- ½ tsp. pepper
- 3 egg yolks, beaten
- 3 egg whites
- 3 tbsp. sliced blanched almonds

Cover the sweetbreads with water and let soak 1 hour. Drain, and place in a saucepan with water to cover; add vinegar. Bring to a boil, and cook 15 minutes. Drain, remove the membrane, plunge the sweetbreads into cold water, and let cool. Drain again and cut into ½-inch cubes. Set aside.

Melt butter in a saucepan, add flour, and stir until smooth. Add cream, salt, and pepper slowly, stirring constantly. Cook until smooth and thick, about 5 minutes. Add the egg yolks and sweetbreads. Mix together well. Correct the seasoning. Preheat oven to moderate, 350°F.

Beat the egg whites until stiff but not dry. Fold them into the sweetbreads mixture carefully. Pour into a buttered 1½-quart soufflé dish. Sprinkle the top with sliced almonds. Bake 30 minutes.

Serve at once.

Florentine Tongue Soufflé

[4 servings]

- 3 slices stale bread, crumbled
- ½ cup milk
- 4 tbsp. butter
- 1 tsp. grated onion
- 1 cup cooked spinach or chard
- ¾ cup coarsely chopped cooked beef tongue
- 1 tsp. salt
- ¼ tsp. pepper
- 3 egg yolks
- 4 egg whites

Soak the crumbled bread in the milk about 15 minutes. Drain well. Melt butter in a saucepan, add the soaked bread and grated onion. Cook over low heat 5 minutes, stirring occasionally.

Drain the spinach or chard, grind it, and add to the bread and onion with the chopped tongue, salt, and pepper. Continue cooking 5 minutes longer, stirring occasionally. Set aside to cool for 5 minutes. Beat the egg yolks until light in color, and gradually add to the tongue mixture, beating constantly. Return the pan to the heat, and cook for 5 minutes more, stirring constantly. Remove from heat, and let cool for 10 minutes. Preheat oven to moderate, 375°F.

Beat the egg whites until stiff but not dry. Fold them into the tongue mixture carefully. Pour into a buttered 1½-quart soufflé dish. Bake 35 minutes.

Serve at once.

SIX

Vegetable Soufflés

A vegetable soufflé, served as an accompaniment to a simple main course, will brighten an otherwise routine meal. You will also be able to utilize leftover vegetables and give them a little glamor.

Served instead of a soup course, soufflés give a great deal of variety to menu planning. The choice of vegetables for soufflés is practically endless, and the combination of flavors may interest even those who do not ordinarily care for vegetables.

Some of the soufflés in this section are ideally suited for luncheon or supper dishes. They should be served with cold meats or poultry, or with sandwiches.

Acorn-Squash Soufflé

[4 to 8 servings]

4 large acorn squashes	½ cup milk, scalded
2 tbsp. butter	1 tsp. salt
1 onion, peeled and sliced	½ tsp. pepper
2 tbsp. sifted all-purpose flour	3 egg yolks, beaten
1 cup stock, *or* 1 cup boiling water and 1 chicken bouillon cube	3 egg whites
	⅛ tsp. cayenne pepper

Wash the squashes, turn each on its flat side, and cut off the top, horizontally. Scoop out the seeds and fibers. Place squashes in a pan containing 2 inches of water, and bake in a moderate oven, 350°F., 1 hour. Remove, let cool for 20 minutes. Scoop out the pulp and mash well. Reserve the shells.

Melt the butter in a saucepan, add onion, and sauté 2 minutes. Add flour, stirring until smooth. Add stock, milk, salt, and pepper gradually, stirring constantly. Bring to boiling point, still stirring continuously, and cook over low heat for 10 minutes, stirring occasionally. This should reduce the cream sauce to about 1 cup. Strain. Combine with the mashed squash, and mix well. Slowly add the egg yolks, stirring steadily. Set aside to cool for 5 minutes. Preheat oven to moderate, 350°F.

Beat the egg whites until stiff but not dry. Fold into the squash mixture carefully. Pour into the squash shells three-quarter full, and sprinkle cayenne over the tops. Bake on a baking sheet 20 minutes.

Serve at once.

Any leftover squash soufflé mixture can be baked in greased custard cups and used as a garnish around the large soufflés.

Asparagus Soufflé

[4 to 6 servings]

- 12 fresh asparagus tips, *or* 1 package frozen asparagus
- 1 cup water
- 1 tsp. salt
- 4 tbsp. butter
- 1 onion, peeled and chopped
- 3 tbsp. sifted all-purpose flour
- 1 cup milk, scalded
- 3 egg yolks, well beaten
- dash cayenne pepper
- 1/4 cup grated Swiss cheese
- 3 egg whites

Boil the asparagus in salted water until tender, but firm, about 15 minutes. Drain, and set aside.

Melt the butter in a saucepan, add onion, and sauté 2 minutes over low heat. Add flour, stirring constantly. Add milk, stirring as you pour. Cook until thick and smooth, about 5 minutes. Let cool for 15 minutes. Add the egg yolks, cayenne, and cheese. Correct the seasoning. Preheat oven to moderate, 350°F.

Beat the egg whites until stiff but not dry. Fold them into the cheese mixture carefully. Pour over asparagus tips in the bottom of a buttered 1½-quart soufflé dish. Bake 35 minutes.

Serve at once.

Asparagus-and-Cheese Soufflé

[4 to 6 servings]

3 tbsp. butter
1 onion, peeled and sliced
3 tbsp. sifted all-purpose flour
1 cup stock, *or* 1 cup boiling water and 1 chicken bouillon cube
1 tsp. salt
dash cayenne pepper
½ cup light cream, scalded
½ cup grated Swiss cheese
3 egg yolks, beaten
1 cup cooked asparagus tips, fresh or frozen
3 egg whites

Melt the butter in a saucepan, add onion, and sauté 2 minutes. Sprinkle with flour, and stir until smooth. Add stock, salt, cayenne, and cream gradually, stirring constantly. Bring to a boil, and cook over low heat 10 minutes, stirring occasionally. This should reduce the cream sauce to about 1 cup. Strain, and let cool for 15 minutes. Add all but 2 tablespoons of cheese and mix well. Add the egg yolks gradually, stirring continuously.

Cut the asparagus into the thinnest slices possible, add to the cheese sauce, stirring well. Preheat oven to moderate, 375°F.

Beat the egg whites until stiff but not dry. Fold them into the asparagus and cheese sauce carefully. Pour into a buttered 1½-quart soufflé dish. Sprinkle with the remaining 2 tablespoons of cheese. Bake 30 minutes.

Serve at once.

Boston-Bean Soufflé

[4 to 6 servings]

1 (1-lb.) can baked beans
½ cup tomato juice
3 egg yolks, beaten
½ tsp. salt
¼ tsp. pepper
½ tsp. dry mustard
dash cayenne pepper
4 frankfurters
4 egg whites

Force the beans through a sieve, or purée them in an electric blender. Combine the purée with the tomato juice. Add the egg yolks, salt, pepper, mustard, and cayenne, and mix well together.

Slice frankfurters into ¼-inch pieces, and fry in a pan 2 minutes. Drain, and add the frankfurters to the bean mixture, reserving about 6 pieces. Preheat oven to moderate, 350°F.

Beat the egg whites until stiff but not dry. Fold them into the frankfurter mixture carefully. Pour into a 1½-quart unbuttered soufflé dish. Place the 6 pieces of frankfurter in a circle on top of the soufflé. Bake 40 minutes.

Serve at once.

Bean-and-Corn Soufflé

[4 to 6 servings]

- 4 tbsp. butter
- 2 tbsp. chopped green pepper
- 3 tbsp. sifted all-purpose flour
- ¾ cup stock, *or* ¾ cup water and 1 bouillon cube
- ¾ cup light cream, scalded
- ¾ cup coarsely chopped cooked green beans
- ¾ cup cooked or canned corn kernels
- 2 tbsp. chopped pimiento
- ½ tsp. salt
- ½ tsp. sugar
- ½ tsp. pepper
- 4 egg yolks, beaten
- 4 egg whites

Melt the butter in a saucepan, add the green pepper and sauté 2 minutes. Sprinkle flour over pepper and stir until smooth. Add stock and cream gradually, stirring constantly. Cook 5 minutes more, stirring occasionally. Add beans, corn, pimiento, salt, sugar, and pepper. Mix well. Add the egg yolks gradually, stirring constantly. Set aside to cool for 15 minutes. Preheat oven to moderate, 350°F.

Beat the egg whites until stiff but not dry. Fold into the vegetable mixture carefully. Pour into an unbuttered 1½-quart soufflé dish. Bake 30 minutes.

Serve at once.

Short-Cut Bean, Tomato, and Bacon Soufflé

[4 to 6 servings]

- 4 egg yolks
- 1 (10½-oz.) can condensed tomato soup
- ¾ cup canned or cooked fresh or frozen lima beans, cut into small pieces
- 6 slices crisp bacon, crumbled
- ½ tsp. salt
- ⅛ tsp. pepper
- 4 egg whites

Beat the egg yolks in a bowl, add the tomato soup gradually, stirring continuously. Add lima beans and all but 1 crumbled slice of bacon, and stir. Add salt and pepper, and mix all well. Preheat oven to moderate, 350°F.

Beat the egg whites until stiff but not dry. Fold them into the bean mixture carefully. Pour into a buttered 1½-quart soufflé dish. Crumble the remaining slice of bacon on top. Bake 30 minutes.

Serve at once.

String-Bean Soufflé

[4 to 6 servings]

- 1 pound string beans, *or* 1 package frozen string beans
- 1 cup boiling water
- 3 tbsp. butter
- 3 tbsp. sifted all-purpose flour
- 1 cup milk, scalded
- 1 tsp. salt
- 2 tbsp. sliced blanched almonds
- 4 egg whites
- 2 tbsp. bread crumbs

Cook the beans in boiling water until very tender, about 30 minutes. Drain; force through a strainer. Set aside.

Melt the butter in a saucepan, add flour. Stir until smooth. Add the milk gradually, stirring as you add. Cook until smooth and thick, stirring constantly. Add the bean purée, and almonds, and mix well. Correct seasoning. Let cool for 10 minutes. Preheat the oven to moderate, 350°F.

Beat the egg whites until stiff but not dry. Fold them into the bean mixture carefully. Pour into a buttered 1½-quart soufflé dish dusted with bread crumbs. Bake 30 minutes.

Serve at once.

Broccoli Soufflé

[4 to 6 servings]

- 6 tbsp. butter
- ¼ cup sifted all-purpose flour
- ½ cup heavy cream, scalded
- ½ cup stock, *or* 1 chicken bouillon cube dissolved in ½ cup boiling water
- 2 tbsp. grated onion
- 2 tsp. chopped parsley
- 1 tsp. salt
- 1 tsp. pepper
- dash cayenne pepper
- 3 egg yolks, beaten
- 1¼ cups chopped cooked broccoli
- ⅓ cup grated Cheddar cheese
- 3 egg whites

Melt butter in a saucepan, add flour, stirring until smooth. Combine cream and stock and add gradually to the flour mixture, stirring continuously until boiling. Cook until smooth and thick, about 5 minutes, stirring occasionally. Add onion, parsley, salt, pepper, and cayenne. Mix well. Let cool for 5 minutes. Gradually add the egg yolks, beating well. Add broccoli and cheese and mix well. Let cool for 15 minutes. Preheat oven to moderate, 375°F.

Beat the egg whites until stiff but not dry. Fold into broccoli mixture carefully. Pour into a buttered 1½-quart soufflé dish. Bake 30 minutes.

Serve at once.

Celery Soufflé, Parmigiana

[4 to 6 servings]

- 1 large bunch celery
- 2 cups stock, *or* 2 cups boiling water and 2 chicken bouillon cubes
- 1 onion, peeled and sliced
- 2 slices bacon
- 4 egg yolks
- 1 (10½-oz.) can condensed tomato soup
- ½ cup grated Parmesan cheese
- 4 egg whites

Wash celery thoroughly, discarding leaves, and chop the stalks coarsely. Cook in the stock, with onion and bacon until tender, about 10 minutes. Drain, and discard liquid, onion, and bacon. Set celery aside to cool for 10 minutes.

Beat the egg yolks in a bowl until light in color. Add tomato soup gradually, beating steadily. Add cheese, mix well, and combine with the celery. Correct seasoning. Preheat oven to moderate, 350°F.

Beat the egg whites until stiff but not dry. Fold them into the celery mixture carefully. Pour into a buttered 1½-quart soufflé dish. Bake 30 minutes.

Serve at once.

Chard Soufflé

[4 to 6 servings]

- 4 tbsp. butter
- ¼ cup sifted all-purpose flour
- 1½ cups milk, scalded
- 1 tsp. salt
- ¼ tsp. pepper
- 1 tsp. Worcestershire sauce
- 1¼ cups chopped cooked chard
- 1 tbsp. grated onion
- 1 tbsp. chopped parsley
- 4 egg yolks
- 4 egg whites
- 1 tbsp. bread crumbs

Melt the butter in a saucepan, add flour, and stir until smooth. Add the milk gradually, stirring constantly until boiling point is reached. Add salt, pepper, and Worcestershire sauce, and cook 5 minutes longer, stirring occasionally. Combine half of this white sauce with the chard, mix well, and correct the seasoning. Butter a 1½-quart soufflé dish, and pour the chard mixture into the dish. Set aside.

To the remaining half of the white sauce, add onion and parsley, and stir. Beat the egg yolks in a bowl until light in color. Add the onion-parsley white sauce gradually, beating constantly. Let cool for 10 minutes. Preheat oven to moderate, 375°F.

Beat the egg whites until stiff but not dry. Fold them into the previous mixture carefully. Pour on top of the chard mixture in the soufflé dish. Sprinkle bread crumbs on top. Bake 35 minutes.

Serve at once.

Chestnut-Ring Soufflé

[4 to 6 servings]

- 1 lb. uncooked chestnuts (1 cup shelled cooked chestnuts)
- ½ cup milk
- 2 tbsp. cornstarch
- 1 tsp. grated onion
- 1 tsp. salt
- ⅛ tsp. pepper
- ⅛ tsp. paprika
- 3 egg whites

Make a crisscross mark with a sharp paring knife on each chestnut. Cook nuts covered with boiling water 30 minutes. Drain, remove shells, and force nuts through a ricer. Let cool for 10 minutes.

Mix milk with cornstarch in a saucepan, cook and stir until smooth; let boil 2 minutes longer.

Mix the chestnuts, onion, salt, pepper, and paprika together. Add the thickened milk slowly to the chestnut purée, beating steadily. Set aside to cool for 10 minutes. Preheat oven to moderate, 350°F.

Beat the egg whites until stiff but not dry. Fold them into the chestnut mixture carefully. Pour into a buttered 7-inch ring mold. Set the mold in a shallow pan of water. Bake 45 minutes.

To unmold, run a knife around the edge, tap the sides gently, and turn out carefully onto a warmed plate.

This soufflé should not be served as a dessert, but as a vegetable or an accompaniment with roast turkey. As a separate course, the center of the ring may be filled with creamed vegetables.

Serve at once.

Corn-and-Cheese Soufflé

[4 to 6 servings]

4 tbsp. butter
3 tbsp. minced green pepper
2 tbsp. sifted all-purpose flour
1¼ cups light cream, scalded
½ cup grated American cheese
3 egg yolks, beaten
1 tsp. salt
½ cup cooked or canned corn kernels
3 tbsp. chopped pimiento
3 egg whites

Melt the butter in a saucepan, add green pepper and sauté lightly 2 minutes. Add flour and stir until smooth. Add cream, stirring constantly. Cook 5 minutes, continuing to stir. Add the cheese and mix well. Remove from the heat, add the egg yolks, salt, corn, and pimiento, stirring all together well. Correct the seasoning. Let cool for 15 minutes. Preheat oven to moderate, 350°F.

Beat the egg whites until stiff, but not dry. Fold them into the cheese mixture carefully. Pour into an unbuttered 1½-quart soufflé dish. Bake 30 minutes.

Serve at once.

Corn-Paprika Soufflé

[4 to 6 servings]

- 2 cups cooked or canned corn kernels
- 3 tbsp. water
- 2 tbsp. butter
- ¼ cup heavy cream
- 1 tsp. paprika
- 1 tsp. salt
- 4 egg yolks, beaten
- 4 egg whites

Combine the corn and water in a saucepan and boil 10 minutes if fresh corn is used, 3 minutes if canned. Drain well, and force corn through a sieve.

Melt the butter in a saucepan, add the sieved corn, and cook over low heat, stirring occasionally, until all the liquid is absorbed, and the corn is dry without being browned. Add cream, paprika, and salt, and stir well. Add the egg yolks gradually, stirring continuously. Remove from heat, and let cool for 10 minutes. Preheat oven to moderate, 375°F.

Beat the egg whites until stiff but not dry. Fold them into the corn mixture carefully. Pour into a buttered 1½-quart soufflé dish, and sprinkle a little paprika on top. Bake 30 minutes.

Serve at once.

Egg-Ring Soufflé

[4 to 6 servings]

6 egg yolks	1¼ tsp. salt
5 tbsp. sifted all-purpose flour	⅔ cup sweet cider
3 tsp. baking powder	6 egg whites

Beat the egg yolks in a bowl until light in color. Sift flour, baking powder, and salt together; add to the yolks, mixing well. Add the cider slowly, stirring continuously. Preheat oven to moderate, 325°F.

Beat the egg whites until stiff but not dry. Fold them into the yolk mixture carefully. Pour into a buttered 9-inch ring mold. Place in a shallow pan of hot water. Bake 45 minutes, or until the soufflé looks firm, and begins to leave the sides of the pan.

Loosen the sides gently with a knife, and unmold onto a warmed plate. The center may be filled with any creamed mixture, such as vegetables or chicken. Also good in this ring soufflé are stewed tomatoes, or chicken, creole style.

Serve at once.

Eggplant Soufflé

[4 to 6 servings]

2 cups cubed pared eggplant
2 cups cubed pared potatoes
1 onion, peeled and sliced
2 cups water
1 sprig parsley
1 bay leaf
2 tsp. salt
1 tsp. pepper
½ cup heavy cream
3 egg yolks, beaten
2 tbsp. bread crumbs
3 egg whites

Combine the eggplant, potatoes, onion, water, parsley, bay leaf, salt, and pepper in a saucepan, cook until the potatoes are soft, about 10 minutes. Remove the bay leaf. Force the vegetables through a ricer. Add the cream, egg yolks, and bread crumbs, mixing well. Let cool 10 minutes. Preheat oven to moderate, 325°F.

Beat the egg whites until stiff but not dry. Fold them into the vegetable mixture carefully. Pour into a 1½-quart buttered soufflé dish. Bake 40 minutes.

Serve at once.

Since this is a bland dish, a Tomato Vinaigrette Sauce is recommended, see page 220.

Eggplant-and-Cheese Soufflé

[4 to 6 servings]

1 medium eggplant
1 cup water
2 tbsp. butter
2 tbsp. sifted all-purpose flour
1 cup milk
1 cup grated Gruyère cheese
¾ cup bread crumbs
½ tsp. salt
¼ tsp. pepper
2 tsp. grated onion
1 tbsp. tomato catsup
2 egg yolks
3 egg whites

Wash the eggplant, pare, and cut into small pieces. Cook in 1 cup water until tender, about 10 minutes. Drain well, and mash. Set aside to cool for 5 minutes.

Melt the butter in a saucepan, add flour, and stir over low heat until smooth. Add milk, stirring constantly; continue cooking until thick and smooth, about 5 minutes, stirring occasionally. Add eggplant, cheese, bread crumbs, salt, pepper, onion, and catsup, and stir. Beat the egg yolks until light in color, and add them gradually to the eggplant mixture, beating constantly. Let cool for 15 minutes. Preheat oven to moderate, 350°F.

Beat the egg whites until stiff but not dry. Fold them carefully into the eggplant mixture. Pour into a buttered 1½-quart soufflé dish. Bake 40 minutes.

Serve as a luncheon entrée, with a green salad.

Serve at once.

Hominy Soufflé

[4 to 6 servings]

1 tsp. salt
1 cup boiling water
¾ cup hominy grits
2 cups milk
3 tbsp. butter, melted
4 egg yolks
5 egg whites

Combine salt and boiling water in the top of a double boiler. Add the grits slowly, stirring constantly. Cook over direct heat 2 minutes, still stirring. Add the milk gradually, mixing well; place over hot water. Cook for 30 minutes. Add the butter and mix well. Correct the seasoning.

Beat the egg yolks in a bowl. Add the hot mixture gradually to the yolks, stirring steadily. Set aside to cool for 15 minutes. Preheat oven to moderate, 350°F.

Beat the egg whites until stiff but not dry. Fold them into the hominy mixture carefully. Pour into a buttered 1½-quart soufflé dish. Bake 45 minutes.

Serve at once.

Hominy-and-Cheese Soufflé

[4 to 6 servings]

1 cup water
1 cup milk
1 tsp. salt
½ cup hominy grits

Combine the water and milk in the upper part of a double boiler. Bring to boiling point over direct heat. Add salt and the grits, stirring constantly, over low heat. Place over hot water, and cook for 45 minutes, stirring occasionally. Remove from the heat and set aside to cool for 15 minutes. Now prepare:

3 egg yolks
6 tbsp. grated Parmesan cheese
½ tsp. salt
¼ tsp. pepper
3 tbsp. butter, melted
4 egg whites

Beat the egg yolks in a bowl until light in color. Add the cooked grits to the yolks, beating steadily until smooth. Add the cheese, salt, pepper, and melted butter. Mix well. Preheat oven to moderate, 325°F.

Beat the egg whites until stiff but not dry. Fold them into the grits mixture carefully. Pour into a buttered 1½-quart soufflé dish. Bake 40 minutes.

Serve at once.

This is an excellent luncheon dish. A tossed green salad is the perfect accompaniment for it.

Mexican-Tamale Soufflé

[4 to 6 servings]

¼ cup corn meal
¼ cup cold water
1 tsp. salt
1 cup boiling water
1 cup canned tomatoes
4 egg yolks, beaten
1 cup canned corn kernels, drained
3 tbsp. chopped green pepper
½ cup chopped ripe olives
1 clove garlic, minced
1 tbsp. chili powder
4 egg whites
1 tbsp. bread crumbs

Mix the corn meal with the cold water; pour gradually into salted boiling water in the top of a double boiler. Place over hot water, stir constantly until smoothly mixed. Cook 40 minutes, stirring often. Set aside to cool (remove from hot water), for 15 minutes.

Force the tomatoes through a sieve, and add to the egg yolks; beat together thoroughly. Add the cooked corn meal and mix well. Add the corn kernels, green pepper, olives, garlic, and chili powder, and mix well. Correct seasoning. Let cool for 5 minutes. Preheat oven to moderate, 350°F.

Beat the egg whites until stiff but not dry. Fold them into the corn mixture carefully. Pour into a buttered 1½-quart soufflé dish, dusted with bread crumbs. Place in a shallow pan of hot water. Bake 40 minutes.

Serve at once.

Serve with hamburgers or meat loaf.

Mint Soufflé

[4 to 8 servings]

1 (#2) can crushed pineapple
1 (4-oz.) glass mint jelly
2 drops green pure food coloring (optional)
4 egg whites
3 tbsp. sifted all-purpose flour
4 grapefruit shells, *or* 8 orange shells

Drain the pineapple; mash the mint jelly, and combine with the pineapple; add coloring, if desired. Preheat oven to moderate, 350°F.

Beat the egg whites until frothy. Then add flour, and continue beating until the whites are stiff. Fold into the mint mixture carefully. Spoon the mixture into the grapefruit or orange shells, about three-quarters full. Place on a buttered baking sheet. Bake grapefruit 20 minutes, or orange shells for 15 minutes.

This soufflé may also be baked in a regular 1½-quart buttered soufflé dish in a 350°F. oven 30 minutes.

Serve at once.

Traditionally, this soufflé is served with roast leg of lamb, or lamb chops.

Mushroom Soufflé

[4 to 6 servings]

1 pound mushrooms
3 tbsp. butter
4 egg yolks, beaten
1 cup light cream
3 tbsp. sifted all-purpose flour
½ tsp. salt
¼ tsp. pepper
4 egg whites

Wash and drain the mushrooms. Dry them; chop coarsely.

Melt the butter in a saucepan, add the mushrooms, and cook over low heat 10 minutes, stirring frequently. Let cool for 15 minutes. Add the egg yolks, stirring as you add.

Combine cream and flour in the top of a double boiler. Cook over hot water until thick, about 10 minutes, stirring occasionally. Add salt, pepper, and mushroom mixture, stirring constantly. Continue cooking for 2 minutes longer, stirring constantly. Correct seasoning. Set aside to cool for 10 minutes. Preheat oven to moderate, 350°F.

Beat the egg whites until stiff but not dry. Fold them into the mushroom mixture carefully. Pour the soufflé into an unbuttered 1½-quart soufflé dish. Bake 25 minutes.

Serve at once.

Olive-and-Mushroom Soufflé

[4 to 6 servings]

½ pound mushrooms
4 tbsp. butter
2 tbsp. chopped onion
½ cup chopped black olives
3 tbsp. sifted all-purpose flour
¾ cup milk, scalded
½ cup stock, *or* ½ cup boiling water and 1 chicken bouillon cube
½ tsp. salt
¼ tsp. pepper
4 egg yolks
4 egg whites

Wash and drain the mushrooms. Dry them; chop coarsely.

Melt 2 tablespoons of the butter in a saucepan, add onion and mushrooms, and sauté lightly 5 minutes, stirring occasionally. Add olives, mix and set aside.

In another saucepan, heat the remaining 2 tablespoons of butter, and add the flour. Stir until smooth. Add the milk and stock slowly, stirring constantly. Cook 5 minutes, stirring occasionally. Add salt and pepper, and mix. Correct seasoning. Set aside to cool for 10 minutes.

Beat the egg yolks until light in color. Add them gradually to the white sauce, beating constantly to prevent curdling. Add the mushroom-and-olive mixture, stirring well. Set aside to cool for 5 minutes. Preheat oven to moderate, 350°F.

Beat the egg whites until stiff but not dry. Fold them into the mushroom mixture carefully. Pour into a buttered soufflé dish. Bake 35 minutes.

Serve at once.

Onion Soufflé

[4 to 6 servings]

6 large onions, peeled and chopped
8 tbsp. butter
1 cup water
¼ cup sifted all-purpose flour
½ cup heavy cream, scalded
1 tsp. salt
½ tsp. pepper
3 egg yolks, beaten
3 egg whites

Melt 4 tablespoons of the butter in a saucepan; add onion, and sauté 2 minutes. Add water, cover, and cook over low heat until the onions are soft, about 10 minutes. Drain onions; reserve the liquid.

Melt the remaining 4 tbsp. butter in a saucepan. Add the flour, and stir until very smooth. Add cream and the liquid reserved from the onions; cook over low heat for 5 minutes, stirring frequently. Add the onions, salt, and pepper, Mix well and set aside to cool for 10 minutes. Add the egg yolks. Blend throughly. Preheat oven to moderate, 325°F.

Beat the egg whites until stiff but not dry. Fold them into the onion mixture carefully. Pour into an unbuttered 1½-quart soufflé dish. Bake 30 minutes.

Serve at once.

Parsnip Soufflé

[4 to 6 servings]

- 2 cups mashed cooked parsnips
- ¾ cup light cream
- 4 egg yolks, beaten
- 2 tbsp. bread crumbs
- 1 tsp. salt
- ¼ tsp. pepper
- 4 egg whites

Combine the hot mashed parsnips with the cream and beat together until very light and fluffy. Add the egg yolks, bread crumbs, salt, and pepper. Beat smoothly together. Correct the seasoning. Let cool. Preheat oven to moderate, 375°F.

Beat the egg whites until stiff but not dry. Fold them into the parsnip mixture carefully. Pour into a buttered 1½-quart soufflé dish, lightly dusted with flour. Bake for 30 minutes.

Serve at once.

Ring Soufflé of Peas

[4 to 6 servings]

1 tbsp. butter
1 tbsp. flour
½ cup milk, scalded
2 cups cooked peas, fresh or frozen
2 tbsp. heavy cream
2 egg yolks, beaten
1 tsp. salt
½ tsp. pepper
2 tsp. onion juice
2 egg whites

Melt the butter in a saucepan, add flour, and stir until smooth. Add milk slowly, stirring constantly for 3 minutes. Remove from heat, and let cool for 5 minutes.

Force peas through a ricer or sieve. Add cream, egg yolks, salt, pepper, and onion juice. Add to the white sauce, and beat all together thoroughly. Let cool for 15 minutes. Preheat oven to low, 275°F.

Beat the egg whites until stiff but not dry. Fold them into the vegetable mixture carefully. Pour into a buttered 9-inch ring mold, and cover with a large pot lid or a piece of aluminum foil. Place in a shallow pan of hot water. Bake 1 hour.

When ready, run a knife around the pan, tap the sides gently, and unmold slowly and carefully onto a warmed plate. Fill the center with creamed vegetables or chicken.

Serve at once.

Mongol Soufflé

[4 to 6 servings]

2 tbsp. butter
1 tbsp. grated onion
2 tbsp. sifted all-purpose flour
1 cup light cream, scalded
4 egg yolks, beaten
1 cup sliced mushrooms, sautéed
1 cup canned small peas, drained
1 tsp. salt
¼ tsp. pepper
4 egg whites
2 tbsp. bread crumbs

Melt butter in a saucepan, add onion, and sauté 2 minutes. Add flour, mix well until smooth. Add the cream gradually, stirring constantly. Cook until thick and smooth, about 5 minutes, stirring occasionally. Set aside to cool for 15 minutes. Add the egg yolks gradually, stirring constantly. Combine mushrooms, peas, salt, and pepper, and add to the cream sauce. Stir well. Preheat oven to moderate, 350°F.

Beat the egg whites until stiff but not dry. Fold them into the mushroom mixture carefully. Pour into a buttered 1½-quart soufflé dish, sprinkled with bread crumbs. Bake 30 minutes.

Serve at once.

Potato Soufflé

[4 to 6 servings]

2 cups hot mashed potatoes
¾ cup heavy cream
1 tsp. salt
1 tbsp. grated onion
dash cayenne pepper
2 tbsp. grated Parmesan cheese
3 egg yolks, beaten
4 egg whites

Combine potatoes, cream, salt, onion, cayenne, and cheese in a saucepan. Mix thoroughly and heat through. Let cool for 5 minutes. Beat the egg yolks into the potato mixture. Set aside to cool for 15 minutes. Preheat oven to moderate, 350°F.

Beat whites until stiff but not dry. Fold them into the potato mixture carefully. Pour into an unbuttered 1½-quart soufflé dish. Bake 35 minutes.

Serve at once.

Potatoes-in-Their-Shells Soufflé

[4 servings]

4 large baking potatoes
2 tbsp. cream
2 tbsp. butter
1 tsp. salt
¼ tsp. pepper
1 tbsp. chopped chives
3 egg yolks, beaten
3 egg whites

Scrub, rinse, and dry the potatoes. Bake in a hot oven, 425°F., until soft, about 1 hour. Remove from oven and let cool 15 minutes. Reduce oven to moderate, 325°F.

Cut off potato tops lengthwise. Remove the pulp, and reserve the potato skins. Put the pulp through a ricer. Mix with the cream, butter, salt, pepper, and chives. Add the egg yolks, beating all together smoothly.

Beat the egg whites until stiff but not dry. Fold them into the potato mixture carefully. Spoon the mixture into the potato skins about two-thirds full and place the potatoes on a buttered baking sheet. Bake 30 minutes. If any mixture remains, bake it in an individual buttered soufflé dish.

Serve at once.

Curried Rice-and-Cheese Soufflé

[4 to 6 servings]

- ¾ cup white wine
- ¾ cup grated Swiss cheese
- ½ tsp. dry mustard
- 1 tsp. salt
- 1 tbsp. butter, melted
- 1 tbsp. grated onion
- 3 egg yolks
- ⅓ cup boiled rice, unsalted
- 2 tsp. curry powder
- 4 egg whites

Heat the wine to boiling point in a saucepan, and remove from the heat. Add cheese, mustard, salt, butter, and onion. Stir well; set aside to cool for 10 minutes.

Beat the egg yolks in a bowl until light in color. Add the cheese mixture gradually, beating constantly to prevent curdling. Add rice and curry powder, and stir well. Correct the seasoning. If desired, additional curry powder may be added, but the strength of the curry will increase with cooking. Let mixture cool for 5 more minutes. Preheat oven to moderate, 350°F.

Beat the egg whites until stiff but not dry. Fold into the rice mixture carefully. Pour into an unbuttered 1½-quart soufflé dish. Bake 30 minutes.

Serve at once.

This soufflé may be served with a green salad, as a luncheon dish, or with a dinner of roast lamb as an accompaniment in place of potatoes.

Wild-Rice-Ring Soufflé

[6 servings]

⅓ cup butter
⅓ cup sifted all-purpose flour
3½ cups stock, *or* 3½ cups canned consommé
2 tsp. salt
½ tsp. pepper
1 cup wild rice
3 egg yolks
3 egg whites

Melt butter in a saucepan, add flour, stirring until smooth. Add stock gradually, stirring constantly until boiling. Add salt, and pepper.

Wash wild rice until thoroughly clean. Remove any imperfect grains. Drain, and place in the top of a double boiler, pour the white sauce into it. Mix well, cover the pan, place over hot water, and cook until the rice is tender and the sauce absorbed, about 40 minutes. Remove pan from hot water, and set aside to cool for 20 minutes. Beat the egg yolks thoroughly, add to the rice, and stir well. Correct the seasoning. Preheat oven to moderate, 375°F.

Beat the egg whites until stiff but not dry. Fold them into the rice mixture carefully. Pour into a buttered 9-inch ring mold. Place in a shallow pan of hot water. Bake 45 minutes.

Remove from oven when ready, run a knife around the edge, tap the sides gently, and unmold carefully onto a warmed plate. If desired, fill center with vegetables.

Serve at once.

Spinach Soufflé

[4 servings]

2 tbsp. butter
2 tbsp. cornstarch
1 cup milk, scalded
¼ cup light cream, scalded
5 egg yolks
1 cup chopped cooked spinach
1 tsp. salt
½ tsp. pepper
5 egg whites
4 poached eggs, soft

Melt butter in a saucepan, add cornstarch, and mix; add milk and cream, stirring constantly. Cook 10 minutes, stirring occasionally. Let cool for 10 minutes.

Beat the egg yolks in a bowl. Add cream sauce slowly, beating steadily. Add the drained spinach, salt, and pepper, and let cool for 10 minutes. Preheat oven to moderate, 350°F.

Beat the egg whites until stiff but not dry. Fold them into the spinach mixture carefully. Pour half into a buttered 1½-quart soufflé dish. Have poached eggs ready; place the 4 eggs carefully on top of the mixture. Pour the remaining soufflé mixture on top of the eggs. Bake 35 minutes.

Serve at once.

Florentine Soufflé

[4 to 6 servings]

1 package frozen spinach
3 tomatoes, chopped
2 hard-cooked eggs, coarsely chopped
2 tbsp. thick sour cream
1 tsp. salt
½ tsp. dry mustard
1 tsp. lemon juice
4 egg yolks, beaten
2 tbsp. butter
¼ cup sifted all-purpose flour
½ cup stock
½ cup milk, scalded
4 egg whites

Cook the spinach, according to instructions on the package. Drain. Chop fine, and mix with tomatoes, hard-cooked eggs, sour cream, salt, mustard, and lemon juice. Mix well. Add the beaten egg yolks gradually, stirring well.

Melt the butter in a saucepan, add flour, and stir until smooth. Gradually add stock and milk, mixing thoroughly. Cook 3 minutes, stirring continuously. Add the spinach mixture, and mix well. Set aside to cool for 15 minutes. Preheat oven to moderate, 350°F.

Beat the egg whites until stiff but not dry. Fold them into the spinach mixture carefully. Pour into a buttered 1½-quart soufflé dish. Bake 35 minutes.

Serve at once.

Succotash Soufflé

[4 to 6 servings]

- 5 tbsp. butter
- 3 onions, peeled and sliced
- 1 tbsp. sifted all-purpose flour
- ½ cup milk, scalded
- 1 tsp. salt
- ¼ tsp. pepper
- ½ tsp. paprika
- 4 egg yolks
- 1½ cups cooked succotash, fresh, frozen, or canned
- 4 strips crisp bacon, crumbled
- 4 egg whites

Melt 3 tablespoons of butter in a saucepan, and sauté the onions 5 minutes, stirring occasionally. Set aside.

Melt the remaining 2 tablespoons of butter in a saucepan, add flour, and stir until smooth. Add the milk gradually, stirring constantly until the mixture boils. Add salt, pepper, and paprika, and stir. Cook over low heat until the mixture is thick and smooth, about 5 minutes, stirring occasionally. Remove from heat.

Beat the egg yolks until light in color. Add the white sauce gradually to the yolks, stirring constantly to prevent curdling. Add the sautéed onions, the succotash, and bacon, and mix well. Let cool for 10 minutes. Preheat oven to moderate, 375°F.

Beat the egg whites until stiff but not dry. Fold them into the onion mixture carefully. Pour into a buttered 1½-quart soufflé dish. Bake 35 minutes.

Serve at once.

Sweet Potato Soufflé

[4 to 6 servings]

2 cups mashed cooked sweet potatoes
⅔ cup scalded milk
¼ cup brandy
1 tsp. salt
2 tsp. sugar
2 tsp. grated orange rind
4 egg yolks
3 tbsp. butter, melted
5 egg whites
2 tbsp. crushed corn flakes

Combine the sweet potatoes, milk, brandy, salt, sugar, and orange rind. Mix well. Beat the egg yolks until light, and add gradually to the mixture, stirring steadily. Add the melted butter, and continue stirring until the mixture is light and fluffy. Preheat oven to moderate, 375°F.

Beat the egg whites until stiff but not dry. Fold them into the potato mixture carefully. Pour into a buttered 1½-quart soufflé dish, sprinkle top with corn flakes. Bake 30 minutes.

Serve at once.

Sweet Potato-and-Cheese Soufflé

[4 to 6 servings]

- 2 lbs. sweet potatoes, pared and cubed, *or* 3 cups leftover or canned sweet potatoes
- 3 tbsp. butter
- 2 tbsp. cornstarch
- 1 cup light cream, scalded
- 4 egg yolks, beaten
- 1 tsp. salt
- ½ tsp. pepper
- 2 tbsp. grated onion
- 1 tbsp. chopped parsley
- 1 tbsp. brandy
- 1 cup grated Swiss cheese
- 4 egg whites
- ¼ cup ground pecans

If raw sweet potatoes are used, place in a pan with just enough water to cover. Bring to boiling point and boil 15 minutes. Drain, mash, and set aside to cool for 15 minutes.

Melt butter in a saucepan, and remove the pan from the heat. Add cornstarch, and stir until smooth. Add the scalded cream gradually, stirring constantly, and return the pan to the heat. Cook 5 minutes, stirring occasionally. Remove pan and let cool for 5 minutes. Add the mashed potatoes, egg yolks, salt, pepper, onion, parsley, brandy, and cheese. Mix together for 1 minute. Preheat oven to moderate, 375°F.

Beat the egg whites until stiff but not dry. Fold them into the potato mixture carefully. Pour into a buttered 1½-quart soufflé dish dusted lightly with half of the ground pecans. Sprinkle the remaining pecans on top. Bake 30 minutes.

Serve at once.

Tomato Soufflé, Normandy

[4 to 6 servings]

- 6 large tomatoes, *or* 2½ cups canned tomatoes
- 1 onion, grated
- 1 bay leaf
- 2 tbsp. butter
- 2 tbsp. sifted all-purpose flour
- 1 tsp. salt
- ¼ tsp. pepper
- ½ cup hot milk
- 3 egg yolks, beaten
- 1 tbsp. brandy
- ½ cup applesauce
- 3 egg whites

Wash, peel and slice the tomatoes. Cook in a saucepan without water 5 minutes over low heat. Add onion and bay leaf. Continue cooking over low heat 10 minutes, being careful not to burn the tomatoes. Remove the bay leaf. Press tomatoes through a sieve. There should be about 2½ cups of tomato pulp. Set aside to cool for 15 minutes.

Melt the butter in a saucepan, add flour, salt, and pepper, and stir until smooth. Add milk gradually, stirring constantly. Bring to a boil, remove from heat, and let cool 10 minutes. Add the tomatoes, and mix well. Add the egg yolks and brandy, beating constantly.

Preheat oven to moderate, 350°F. Spread the applesauce on the bottom of an unbuttered 1½-quart soufflé dish.

Beat the egg whites until stiff but not dry. Fold them into the tomato mixture carefully. Pour over the applesauce in the soufflé dish. Bake 30 minutes.

Serve at once.

Quick Tomato Soufflé

[4 to 6 servings]

1 (10½-oz.) can condensed tomato soup
1 bay leaf
2 chicken bouillon cubes
¼ cup grated Swiss cheese
4 egg yolks
1 (#2) can macaroni and cheese
4 egg whites
2 tbsp. grated Parmesan cheese

Heat the soup in a saucepan, add bay leaf, and dissolve chicken bouillon cubes in the soup. Cook 3 minutes; remove the bay leaf. Add the Swiss cheese, and stir well. Set aside to cool for 15 minutes.

Beat the egg yolks and add to the soup mixture gradually, stirring as you add. Preheat oven to moderate, 375°F.

Butter a 2-quart soufflé dish, and pour the macaroni-and-cheese in the bottom.

Beat the egg whites until stiff, but not dry. Fold them into the soup mixture carefully. Pour on top of the macaroni-and-cheese in the soufflé dish. Sprinkle the Parmesan cheese on the soufflé. Bake 35 minutes.

Serve at once.

Vichyssoise Soufflé

[4 to 6 servings]

6 tbsp. butter
3 leeks, sliced
2 potatoes, pared and cubed
1 sprig parsley
2 cups stock, *or* 2 cups boiling water and 2 chicken bouillon cubes
3 tbsp. sifted all-purpose flour
½ cup light cream
1 tsp. salt
1 tsp. Worcestershire sauce
¼ tsp. pepper
3 egg yolks, beaten
3 egg whites

Melt 3 tablespoons of the butter in a saucepan, and add the leeks. Cook over low heat 10 minutes, but do not let leeks brown. Add potatoes, parsley, and stock. Bring to boiling point, and cook 20 minutes, stirring occasionally. Remove parsley. Strain, reserving 1 cup of the stock. Force the leeks and potatoes through the sieve. Set aside.

Melt the remaining 3 tablespoons of butter in a saucepan, and add flour, stirring well until smooth. Add the cup of strained stock and the cream gradually. Add salt, Worcestershire sauce, and pepper, stirring constantly. Continue cooking until boiling, stirring occasionally. Remove from heat, and let cool for 5 minutes.

Add the puréed potatoes and leeks. Mix; add the egg yolks, beating constantly to prevent curdling. Let cool for 10 minutes. Preheat oven to moderate, 375°F.

Beat the egg whites until stiff but not dry. Fold them into the vegetable mixture carefully. Pour into a buttered 1½-quart soufflé dish. If desired, chives may be sprinkled on top. Bake 30 minutes.

Serve at once.

SEVEN

Dessert Soufflés

Many fine restaurants feature dessert soufflés on their à la carte menu at high prices. Three or four dollars for a soufflé for two persons, is the usual charge. And yet you can serve your family and guests with the same delicious desserts, and at much less.

In this section you will find a wide assortment of dessert soufflés inspired by practically every fruit and flavor that you are likely to encounter. With just a little practice, you should be able to produce perfect soufflés every time.

Always follow the instructions on how to fold in the egg whites; reread the introduction, because the folding in of the egg whites is more important in a delicate dessert soufflé than with any other kind. Here, lightness and delicacy of flavor should be at their best.

A sprinkling of granulated or confectioners' sugar on top of a dessert soufflé will give it an extra gloss, and the finished soufflé will be a little sweeter and have an unusual cakelike exterior.

Many recipes suggest a sauce to be served with the soufflé. However, whipped cream is a general favorite with a dessert soufflé.

Almond Soufflé

[4 servings]

3 tbsp. butter
3 tbsp. sifted all-purpose flour
1 cup milk, scalded
¼ cup sugar
¾ cup ground blanched almonds
¾ tsp. almond extract
2 tbsp. brandy
4 egg yolks, beaten
4 egg whites

Melt the butter in a saucepan, add flour, stir until smooth. Add the milk gradually, stirring constantly. Add sugar, and cook over low heat, stirring constantly until the boiling point. Cook until thick and smooth. Add the almonds, almond extract, and brandy, and mix together well. Pour this mixture gradually into the egg yolks in a bowl, stirring constantly to prevent curdling. Set aside to cool for 15 minutes. Preheat oven to moderate, 375°F.

Beat the egg whites until stiff but not dry. Fold them into the almond mixture carefully. Pour into a buttered 1½-quart soufflé dish dusted with sugar. Bake 40 minutes.

Serve at once.

Almond-Macaroon Soufflé

[4 servings]

1 package vanilla pudding
2 tbsp. sugar
½ cup milk
½ cup light cream
4 egg yolks
8 macaroons, crumbled fine
½ cup ground blanched almonds
½ tsp. almond extract
dash salt
5 egg whites

Combine the vanilla pudding with sugar, milk, and cream in a saucepan. Cook over low heat, stirring constantly, until thick and smooth, or about 5 minutes. Let cool for 5 minutes.

Beat the egg yolks until light in color; add to the cream mixture gradually, beating steadily to prevent curdling. Combine macaroon crumbs with almonds, add to the egg mixture and stir. Add the almond extract, and stir again. Set aside to cool for 20 minutes. Preheat oven to moderate, 350°F.

Sprinkle the salt on the egg whites, and beat until stiff but not dry. Fold them into the macaroon mixture carefully. Pour into an unbuttered 1½-quart soufflé dish. If desired, some macaroon crumbs or ground almonds, or both, may be sprinkled on top. Bake 40 minutes.

Serve at once.

Almond-Sponge Soufflé

[6 servings]

5 tbsp. butter
5 tbsp. sugar
6 egg yolks, beaten
1 cup grated blanched almonds
1/8 tsp. salt
1 tsp. vanilla extract
1 tbsp. brandy
6 egg whites

Cream the butter well, add the sugar, and beat smoothly together. Add the egg yolks gradually, stirring constantly. Add almonds, salt, vanilla, and brandy, and beat all together very well.

Beat the egg whites until stiff but not dry. Fold them into the almond mixture carefully. Pour into the buttered top of a 2-quart double boiler, sprinkled lightly with sugar. Place over, but not touching, hot water, and *cover*. Cook 1 hour.

Run a knife around the edge and turn out onto a warmed plate.

Serve at once.

Apple Soufflé

[4 servings]

- 4 egg yolks
- ⅔ cup brown sugar (packed)
- 1½ cups applesauce
- 2 tbsp. brandy
- 1 tbsp. grated orange rind
- 2 tbsp. granulated sugar
- 4 egg whites

Beat the egg yolks in a bowl until light in color. Add brown sugar, and beat until well blended. Drain applesauce of all juice. Combine with brandy, orange rind, and granulated sugar. Add to the yolk mixture, and stir well. Preheat oven to moderate, 350°F.

Beat the egg whites until stiff but not dry. Fold them into the apple mixture carefully. Pour into a buttered 1½-quart soufflé dish. Sprinkle sugar on top. Bake 30 minutes.

Serve at once.

Serve with Brown-Sugar Sauce, see page 224.

Baked-Apple Soufflé

[4 servings]

3 baking apples
5 tbsp. brown sugar
3 tbsp. granulated sugar
1 tbsp. sifted all-purpose flour
4 egg yolks, beaten
1 cup milk
2 tbsp. brandy
5 egg whites

Wash and pare apples, sprinkle with brown sugar, and place on a greased baking sheet. Bake in a moderate, 350°F. oven 20 minutes. Remove apples. Set aside to cool for 15 minutes. Core apples and cut in thick slices. Reduce oven temperature to 375°F.

Combine granulated sugar, flour, and egg yolks in a saucepan, beating until well mixed. Add milk gradually, stirring steadily; cook over low heat, continuing to stir until thick and smooth, about 5 minutes. Remove from the heat, add the brandy, and let cool for 10 minutes.

Beat the egg whites until stiff but not dry. Fold them into the yolk mixture carefully. Pour half of the soufflé mixture into a buttered 1½-quart soufflé dish. Place the cooled slices of baked apples on top of the soufflé, and pour the remainder of the soufflé mixture on top of the apples. Sprinkle a little sugar on top. Bake 20 minutes.

Serve at once.

Serve with Brandied Whipped Cream, see page 230.

Apricot Soufflé

[4 servings]

5 egg whites
5 tbsp. sifted brown sugar
¾ cup apricot purée (canned or strained baby food)
dash salt
½ tsp. vanilla extract

Butter a 1½-quart soufflé dish, and sprinkle lightly with sugar. Preheat oven to moderate, 350°F.

Beat the egg whites until stiff but not dry. Add brown sugar and beat lightly again until well mixed. Fold in the apricot purée slowly and gently. Add salt and vanilla. Pour soufflé mixture into prepared dish, and sprinkle a little more sugar on top. Place the dish in a shallow pan of hot water. Bake 30 minutes.

Serve at once.

Fresh Apricot Soufflé

[4 servings]

1 cup mashed fresh apricots (5 or 6 apricots)
½ cup sugar
1 tsp. orange juice
1 tsp. lemon juice
5 egg whites
1 tbsp. ground almonds

Wash, peel, and remove pits from apricots. Force apricots through a sieve. Combine with sugar in a saucepan, and cook over low heat until the sugar is completely melted, stirring frequently. Add orange and lemon juice, stir and remove from heat. Set aside to cool for 15 minutes. Preheat oven to moderate, 325°F.

Butter a 1½-quart soufflé dish, and dust with sugar lightly.

Beat the egg whites until stiff but not dry. Fold them into the apricot mixture carefully. Pour into the soufflé dish, sprinkle ground almonds on top. Bake 40 minutes.

Serve at once.

Serve with Raspberry Sauce, see page 228.

Avocado Soufflé

[4 servings]

- 3 tbsp. butter
- 2 tbsp. sifted all-purpose flour
- 1 cup light cream, scalded
- 4 egg yolks, beaten
- ¼ cup sugar
- ½ tsp. salt
- 1 cup mashed avocado
- 1 tbsp. lemon juice
- 4 egg whites

Melt the butter in a saucepan, add flour, and stir until smooth. Add cream gradually, stirring constantly. Continue cooking and stirring over low heat, until thickened, or about 5 minutes. Let cool for 5 minutes. Add the egg yolks gradually, stirring continuously. Add sugar and salt, and stir.

In another bowl, combine the avocado and lemon juice; add to the egg sauce. Mix well. Set aside to cool for another 15 minutes. Preheat oven to moderate, 350°F.

Beat the egg whites until stiff but not dry. Fold them into the avocado mixture carefully. Pour into an unbuttered 1½-quart soufflé dish. Bake 40 minutes.

Serve at once.

Serve with Lemon Sauce, see page 227.

Banana Soufflé

[4 servings]

6 ripe bananas
7 tbsp. confectioners' sugar
1 tbsp. lemon juice
1 tsp. vanilla extract
¼ tsp. salt
4 egg whites

Peel bananas, mash fruit smoothly. Combine with sugar, lemon juice, and vanilla, mixing thoroughly. Preheat oven to moderate, 325°F. Butter a 1½-quart soufflé dish, and sprinkle with a little sugar.

Sprinkle the salt on the egg whites, and beat until stiff but not dry. Fold them into the banana mixture carefully. Pour the soufflé into the dish and sprinkle a little more sugar on top. Place the dish in a shallow pan of hot water. Bake 30 minutes.

Serve at once.

Serve with Chocolate Sauce, see page 225.

Bananas-in-the-Skin Soufflé

[4 servings]

- 4 large bananas
- 1 tbsp. rum
- ½ tbsp. lemon juice
- 1 cup milk, scalded
- 1 tbsp. sugar
- 1 tbsp. sifted all-purpose flour
- 1½ tbsp. butter, melted
- 2 egg yolks, beaten
- 3 egg whites
- 2 tbsp. almond slivers

Select straight, firm, large bananas, not too ripe. Cut off ends, then cut fruit in half lengthwise; remove the interior and put the skins aside. Force the fruit through a sieve; add rum and lemon juice, and mix together. Set aside.

Combine about 1 tablespoon of the milk with the sugar and flour in a saucepan; stir together to make a smooth paste. Gradually stir in the rest of the milk. Bring to a boil over low heat, stirring constantly. Continue cooking until thick and smooth, about 5 minutes longer. Add the banana pulp, melted butter, and the egg yolks, stirring well. Remove and let cool for 10 minutes. Preheat oven to hot, 400°F.

Beat the egg whites until stiff but not dry. Fold them into the banana mixture carefully. Place the banana skins on a flat, buttered pan, and fill each skin about two-thirds full of the soufflé mixture. Sprinkle almond slivers and a little sugar on top of each. Bake 10 minutes.

Serve at once.

Blueberry Soufflé

[4 servings]

2 cups blueberries, fresh or frozen
1 cup sugar
3 tbsp. water
1 tbsp. brandy
2 tsp. grated lemon rind
6 egg whites
2 tbsp. ground blanched almonds

Wash and dry the berries, and press through a sieve; set aside. Boil the sugar and water together in a saucepan until a thread forms when the spoon is lifted to drain above the pan. Add the blueberry pulp, and mix well. Let cool for 30 minutes. It should be cold when combined with beaten whites. Add the brandy and lemon rind, and stir. Preheat oven to moderate, 375°F. Butter a 1½-quart soufflé dish, and sprinkle with sugar.

Beat the egg whites until stiff but not dry. Fold them into the berry mixture carefully. Pour soufflé mixture into the dish, and dust with almonds.

Bake 30 minutes.

Serve at once.

This may be served with whipped cream in which you have mixed a few blueberries.

Candied-Fruit Soufflé

[4 to 6 servings]

1 cup blanched almonds
½ pound butter, plus 2 tbsp.
6 egg yolks
⅓ cup crumbled vanilla cookies, *or* cake crumbs
¼ cup chopped candied fruit
2 tbsp. sugar
1 tsp. vanilla extract
dash of mace, *or* cinnamon
dash salt
6 egg whites

Brown almonds slightly in 2 tablespoons of the butter. Let cool; grind them or chop fine.

Cream the ½ pound of butter until smooth; add the egg yolks one at a time, mixing thoroughly. Add crumbs, almonds, candied fruit, sugar, vanilla, mace or cinnamon, and salt. Mix well. Preheat oven to moderate, 350°F. Butter a 2-quart soufflé dish, and sprinkle lightly with sugar.

Beat the egg whites until stiff but not dry. Fold them into the almond-fruit mixture carefully. Pour into the soufflé dish. Bake 35 minutes.

Serve at once.

Serve with Raspberry Sauce, see page 228, or with whipped cream.

Cherry-Cordial Soufflé

[4 servings]

- 3/8 cup sugar
- 5 egg yolks
- 3/8 cup sifted all-purpose flour
- 1 cup milk, scalded
- 1 cup heavy cream, scalded
- 1/4 cup cherry cordial
- 5 egg whites
- 1/4 tsp. salt

Cream the sugar and the egg yolks together in the top of a double boiler. Stir in the flour and mix well. Add the milk and cream slowly, stirring constantly. Place over hot water, and cook, stirring continuously, until the mixture is thick and smooth, about 5 minutes. Add the cordial, and stir. Remove from the heat and let cool for 10 minutes. Stir occasionally while cooling. Preheat oven to moderate, 350°F.

Butter a 1½-quart soufflé dish, and dust with sugar.

Beat the egg whites with the salt until stiff but not dry. Fold into the soufflé mixture carefully. Pour into the soufflé dish. Bake 30 minutes.

Serve at once.

Cherry Soufflé I

[4 to 6 servings]

- 3 tbsp. sugar
- 3 tbsp. potato flour
- ¼ cup cold milk
- ¾ cup light cream, scalded
- 4 egg yolks, beaten
- 2 tbsp. cherry brandy
- ¾ cup cherry jam
- 5 egg whites

Combine sugar and potato flour in a saucepan, mix. Add the cold milk gradually, and stir together until smooth. Add cream slowly, stirring steadily until the mixture is smooth. Cook over low heat 10 minutes, stirring frequently. Add egg yolks gradually, stirring constantly. Add cherry brandy and jam, and mix again. Remove from the heat, and let cool for 15 minutes. Preheat oven to moderate, 350°F. Butter a 1½-quart soufflé dish, and dust with sugar.

Beat the egg whites until stiff but not dry. Fold them into the cherry mixture carefully. Pour into the soufflé dish. Bake 30 minutes.

Serve at once.

Although this soufflé is rather sweet, it may be served with whipped cream, flavored with a tablespoon of cherry brandy.

Cherry Soufflé II

[4 servings]

1½ cups drained canned Bing cherries, pitted
2 tbsp. sugar
2 tbsp. cherry brandy
6 egg whites
1 cup heavy cream

Reserve 10 cherries. Press the rest of the fruit through a sieve. There should be about 1 cup of cherry purée. Add the sugar and brandy, and mix well. Preheat oven to moderate, 350°F.

Butter a 1½-quart soufflé dish, and sprinkle with sugar.

Beat the egg whites until stiff but not dry. Fold them into the cherry mixture carefully. Pour soufflé into the buttered dish and sprinkle a little sugar on top. Bake 35 minutes.

Serve at once.

Whip cream; add the reserved cherries which may be whole or chopped, and serve with the soufflé.

Chestnut-Dessert Soufflé

[4 servings]

1 lb. uncooked chestnuts
(1 cup shelled cooked chestnuts)
3 egg yolks
¾ cup sugar
¼ tsp. nutmeg
1 tsp. vanilla extract
4 egg whites

Make a crisscross mark with a sharp paring knife on each chestnut. Cook nuts covered with boiling water 30 minutes. Drain, remove the shells, and force through a ricer, sieve, or food mill. Let cool for 10 minutes.

Beat the egg yolks until light in color. Add sugar gradually, beating steadily. Add nutmeg and vanilla, and stir. Add the cooled chestnut purée gradually, beating steadily until smooth. Preheat oven to moderate, 325°F.

Beat the egg whites until stiff but not dry. Fold them into the chestnut mixture carefully. Pour into a 1½-quart buttered and sugared soufflé dish, and sprinkle sugar on top. Bake 40 minutes.

Serve at once.

Serve with whipped cream and Caramel Sauce, see page 224.

Chocolate Soufflé

[4 servings]

½ cup sifted all-purpose flour
½ cup cold milk
½ cup light cream, hot
½ cup sugar
4 egg yolks
dash salt
2 squares (2 oz.) unsweetened chocolate
2 tbsp. water
4 egg whites

Mix the flour and cold milk together until smooth. Add gradually to the hot cream in a saucepan, stirring steadily. Add sugar and cook over low heat about 5 minutes, stirring constantly until thick. Remove from heat, and add the egg yolks, one at a time, beating constantly; add the salt.

Melt the chocolate in the water, using a double boiler; add to the milk mixture. Mix well. Preheat oven to moderate, 350°F.

Butter a 1½-quart soufflé dish, and dust with sugar.

Beat the egg whites until stiff but not dry. Fold into the chocolate mixture. Pour into the soufflé dish. Bake 25 minutes.

Serve at once.

Serve with Foamy Sauce, see page 226.

Bitter-Chocolate Soufflé

[4 to 6 servings]

- 2 squares (2 oz.) unsweetened chocolate
- 3 tbsp. butter
- ½ cup sugar
- 2 egg yolks, beaten
- 1 tsp. vanilla extract
- 1¼ cups sifted all-purpose flour
- 1 tsp. baking powder
- ¼ tsp. salt
- ½ cup light cream
- 3 egg whites

Place chocolate in a cup or upper part of double boiler over hot water, and let melt. Remove from water and let cool for 10 minutes. Cream butter and sugar together. Add the egg yolks, chocolate, and vanilla. Mix well. Sift flour, baking powder, and salt together into the chocolate mixture gradually, alternating with the cream, until all ingredients are well blended.

Butter the top of a 2-quart double boiler carefully.

Beat the egg whites until stiff but not dry. Fold them into the chocolate mixture carefully. Pour into the top of the double boiler and *cover*. Place over, but not touching, hot water, and cook 1½ hours. When ready, run a knife around the edge of the soufflé carefully, tap the sides of the pan gently, and turn out carefully onto a warmed plate.

Serve at once.

Chocolate-Bits Soufflé

[4 servings]

4-oz. package semisweet chocolate bits
1 cup milk
3 egg yolks
¼ cup sugar
⅛ tsp. salt
1 tsp. vanilla extract
3 egg whites

Combine the chocolate and milk in the top of a double boiler, over hot water. When chocolate has melted, beat with a rotary beater for 1 minute while still over hot water. Beat the egg yolks until light. Add sugar and salt. Pour a little of the chocolate mixture into the egg yolks slowly, stirring constantly to prevent curdling, then pour egg mixture into the chocolate mixture, stirring steadily for 1 minute. Add vanilla, and let cool for 15 minutes.

Butter the top of a 1½-2-quart double boiler carefully.

Beat the egg whites until stiff but not dry. Fold them into the chocolate mixture. Pour into the double boiler and cover. Place over, but not touching, hot water, and cook 45 minutes. When ready, run a knife around the edge of the soufflé; tap the sides gently and turn out carefully onto a warmed plate.

Serve at once.

Serve with Coffee Sauce, see page 226.

Chocolate Soufflé, Saxon

[4 servings]

2 squares (2 oz.) unsweetened chocolate
5 egg whites
½ cup sugar
½ cup ground nuts
1 cup whipped cream

Place chocolate in a cup over hot water, and let melt. Remove, and let cool for 10 minutes. Butter the top of a 2-quart double boiler carefully, making sure that the bottom and sides are well greased.

Beat the egg whites until stiff. Add sugar gradually, beating well. Add melted chocolate slowly, stirring constantly until the mixture is well blended. Add nuts, and stir again. Pour into double boiler.* *Cover,* and place over, but not touching, hot water, and cook for 50 minutes.

When ready, run a knife around the edge of the soufflé, tap the sides of the pan gently, and turn out carefully onto a warmed plate. Decorate with whipped cream as quickly as possible.

Serve at once.

* A 2-quart soufflé dish may be used. Butter it very well; *cover* the dish with a pie pan, or aluminum foil. Place in a shallow pan of hot water, and cook 50 minutes on top of the stove.

Fluffy Chocolate Soufflé

[4 servings]

3 oz. sweet chocolate, grated
2 tbsp. cold coffee
6 egg whites
dash salt
¼ cup sugar

Combine chocolate and coffee in a bowl or upper part of double boiler, place over hot water, and stir until melted. Let cool for 10 minutes. Preheat oven to moderate, 350°F. Butter a 1½-quart soufflé dish.

Beat the egg whites until stiff but not dry. Add a dash of salt, and gradually add sugar, beating steadily. Fold in the chocolate slowly but thoroughly, mixing for at least 1 minute. Pour into the soufflé dish. Bake 30 minutes.

Serve at once.

Serve with Foamy Sauce, see page 226.

Chocolate-Tapioca Soufflé

[4 servings]

- 1/3 cup quick-cooking tapioca
- 1/2 cup sugar
- dash salt
- 1 3/4 cups milk
- 2 oz. sweet chocolate
- 1/4 cup coffee, freshly brewed
- 4 egg yolks
- 1 tsp. vanilla extract
- 4 egg whites

Combine tapioca, sugar, salt, and milk in a saucepan. Cook over low heat until the boiling point, stirring constantly. Remove from the heat.

In another saucepan, melt chocolate in the coffee over low heat, stirring until completely melted. Combine with the tapioca mixture; let cool for 10 minutes.

Beat the egg yolks in a bowl until light in color. Add the tapioca-and-chocolate mixture gradually, beating constantly. Add vanilla, and stir. Let cool for 10 additional minutes. Preheat oven to moderate, 350°F.

Butter a 1 1/2-quart soufflé dish and sprinkle lightly with sugar.

Beat the egg whites until stiff but not dry. Fold them into the chocolate mixture carefully. Pour mixture into the soufflé dish. Bake 30 minutes.

Serve at once.

Serve with Foamy Sauce, see page 226.

Short-Cut Chocolate Soufflé

[4 servings]

2 cups milk
1 package chocolate pudding mix
1 tbsp. sugar
dash salt
4 egg yolks
2 tsp. vanilla extract
1 tbsp. grated orange rind
2 tbsp. chocolate bits *or* coarsely broken chocolate
4 egg whites

Combine the milk and pudding mix in a saucepan, and stir smoothly together. Add sugar and salt. Cook over low heat 5 minutes, stirring constantly; the mixture should be very smooth. Set aside to cool for 15 minutes. Beat the egg yolks until light in color. Gradually add the chocolate mixture to the yolks, beating steadily. Add vanilla and orange rind, and stir. Let cool for 5 minutes. Add chocolate bits, and stir. Preheat oven to moderate, 350°F.

Beat the egg whites until stiff but not dry. Fold them into the chocolate mixture carefully. Pour into an unbuttered 1½-quart soufflé dish. Bake 30 minutes.

Serve at once.

Black-and-White Soufflé

[4 servings]

3 tbsp. butter
3 tbsp. sifted all-purpose flour
¾ cup milk, scalded
⅓ cup sugar
dash salt
4 egg yolks
1 tsp. vanilla extract
1 square (1 oz.) unsweetened chocolate, melted and cooled
4 egg whites

Melt the butter in a saucepan, add flour, and stir until smooth. Add milk gradually, stirring constantly. Add sugar and salt, and cook over low heat 5 minutes, stirring constantly.

Beat the egg yolks in a bowl until light in color. Add the hot mixture slowly to the yolks, beating constantly to prevent curdling. Add vanilla, and stir.

Pour half of the egg mixture into another bowl. Add the cooled, melted chocolate, mix well and let cool for 10 minutes. Preheat oven to moderate, 350°F. Butter a 1½-quart soufflé dish, and sprinkle with sugar.

Beat the egg whites until stiff but not dry. Fold half of the whites carefully into the chocolate mixture. Pour into the soufflé dish. Fold the remaining half of the whites carefully into the vanilla mixture. Pour slowly over the chocolate mixture in the soufflé dish. Bake 35 minutes.

Serve at once.

Serve with Milk Chocolate Sauce, see page 225.

Marbleized Soufflé

[4 servings]

- 5 tbsp. butter
- 5 tbsp. sifted all-purpose flour
- 1¼ cups light cream, scalded
- ½ cup sugar
- 1 tsp. vanilla extract
- 5 egg yolks
- 1 square (1 oz.) unsweetened chocolate
- 2 tbsp. strong coffee
- dash salt
- 5 egg whites
- 2 tbsp. grated sweet chocolate

Over low heat, melt butter in a saucepan, and add flour. Stir until smooth. Add cream and sugar gradually, stirring constantly, until thick and smooth, about 5 minutes. Add vanilla and mix. Remove from heat. Beat the egg yolks in a bowl and gradually add the hot mixture, beating constantly. Set aside to cool for 5 minutes.

Place unsweetened chocolate and coffee in a saucepan, over low heat, and stir until dissolved. Let cool for 10 minutes. Preheat oven to moderate, 350°F.

Sprinkle the salt on the egg whites, and beat until stiff but not dry. Fold them into the egg yolk mixture carefully. Using care, fold in the chocolate mixture in a circular effect. Make 3 or 4 turns with the spoon to do this.

Pour into a 1½-quart buttered soufflé dish. Sprinkle the grated sweet chocolate on top. Bake 35 minutes.

Serve at once.

Cinnamon Soufflé

[6 servings]

1 cup sugar
¾ cup water
¼ cup brandy
⅓ cup ground almonds
1½ tsp. powdered cinnamon
¼ tsp. salt
6 egg yolks, beaten
6 egg whites

Combine the sugar, water, and brandy in the top of a double boiler. Cook over hot water, stirring constantly until sugar melts, and syrup thickens, about 15 minutes. Add almonds, but reserve 1 tablespoon. Add cinnamon and salt, and mix well. Let cool for 5 minutes. Beat in the egg yolks gradually, mixing steadily. Let cool for 15 minutes. Preheat oven to moderate, 350°F.

Butter a 1½-quart soufflé dish, and dust with almonds.

Beat the egg whites until stiff but not dry. Fold them into the cinnamon mixture carefully. Pour into the soufflé dish. Place in a shallow pan of hot water. Bake 30 minutes.

Serve at once.

Cocoa-Brandy Soufflé

[6 servings]

- 1 cup milk
- ⅜ cup cocoa
- ⅔ cup sugar
- 4 tbsp. butter
- ⅜ cup sifted all-purpose flour
- 6 egg yolks, beaten
- 6 tbsp. brandy
- dash salt
- 1 tsp. vanilla extract
- 7 egg whites

Combine the milk, cocoa, and sugar in the top of a double boiler. Cook 20 minutes over hot water, stirring occasionally. Remove from heat.

In another saucepan, melt the butter, stir in the flour until smooth. Add the cocoa-and-milk mixture gradually, stirring constantly until thick and smooth. Remove from the heat and let cool for 10 minutes. Gradually add the egg yolks, stirring well. Add the brandy, salt, and vanilla. Stir. Preheat oven to moderate, 375°F.

Beat the egg whites until stiff but not dry. Fold them into the cocoa mixture carefully. Pour into an unbuttered 2-quart soufflé dish. Bake 30 minutes.

Serve at once.

Coffee Soufflé

[4 servings]

- 4 egg yolks, beaten
- ½ cup sugar
- ¼ cup sifted all-purpose flour
- ¾ cup milk
- ¾ cup strongly brewed coffee
- 1 tsp. coffee extract
- 5 egg whites

Combine the egg yolks with the sugar in a saucepan. Continue beating until light in color. Stir in flour, and mix well until blended. Add milk and coffee gradually, stirring constantly. Cook over low heat until the boiling point. Remove from the heat immediately. Add coffee extract. Strain the mixture. Set aside to cool for 15 minutes. Preheat oven to moderate, 325°F. Butter a 1½-quart soufflé dish, and sprinkle with sugar.

Beat the egg whites until stiff but not dry. Fold them into the coffee mixture carefully. Pour into the soufflé dish, and sprinkle a little sugar over the top. If desired, some pulverized coffee may also be sprinkled on the top. Bake 35 minutes.

Serve at once.

Serve with Chocolate Sauce, see page 225.

Coffee-Cream Soufflé

[4 servings]

- 4 egg yolks
- 3/8 cup powdered sugar
- 1 cup (8 oz.) cream cheese
- 1 cup (8 oz.) cottage cheese
- 1½ tbsp. instant-coffee powder
- ¼ cup boiling water
- 1 tbsp. cornstarch
- 2 pieces zwieback, grated
- 4 egg whites

Beat the egg yolks and sugar together until light in color, and thick. Force the cream and cottage cheeses through a sieve, and mix smoothly. Dissolve the instant coffee in the boiling water. Set aside and allow to cool for 10 minutes. Combine the egg and cheese mixtures. Add cornstarch, and stir until well mixed. Add the coffee gradually, stirring constantly. Preheat oven to moderate, 350°F. Butter a 1½-quart soufflé dish very well, and dust with zwieback crumbs.

Beat the egg whites until stiff but not dry. Fold them into the coffee mixture carefully. Pour into the dish. Bake 45 minutes.

Serve at once.

Cranberry Soufflé

[4 to 6 servings]

3 tbsp. lemon juice
1 cup sugar
2 cups uncooked cranberries, ground
½ orange rind, grated
dash salt
4 egg yolks, beaten
4 egg whites

Combine the lemon juice with the sugar in an enamel or glass saucepan, and cook over low heat, stirring constantly, until the sugar melts. Add the cranberries, and cook for 3 minutes longer, stirring occasionally. Add orange rind and salt, and mix well. Set aside to cool for 10 minutes. Add the egg yolks slowly to the fruit mixture, beating steadily. Preheat oven to moderate, 325°F.

Beat the egg whites until stiff but not dry. Fold them into the fruit mixture carefully. Pour into a buttered 1½-quart soufflé dish. Bake 45 minutes.

Serve at once.

This dish may be served as an accompaniment to roast turkey, or as a dessert. For dessert, top it with whipped cream.

Cream Soufflé

[6 to 8 servings]

8 egg yolks, beaten
⅜ cup sugar
1 tsp. vanilla extract
1 cup heavy cream
8 egg whites
2 tbsp. sifted all-purpose flour
⅛ tsp. salt
18 ladyfingers

Cream the egg yolks and sugar together in the upper part of a double boiler until frothy. Add vanilla. Set over hot water. Add the cream, stirring constantly, and cook until thick and smooth, about 15 minutes. Remove the pan from the hot water, and set aside to cool for 15 minutes.

Preheat oven to moderate, 325°F. Line a buttered 2-quart soufflé dish with the ladyfingers.

Beat the egg whites, flour, and salt together until stiff. Combine with the cream mixture carefully. Pour into the soufflé dish. Place dish in a shallow pan of hot water. Bake 35 minutes.

Serve at once.

Mix whipped cream with a few tablespoons of chopped candied fruit, and serve as a sauce with this soufflé.

Cream-Cheese Soufflé

[4 to 6 servings]

- 9 ounces cream cheese
- ¼ cups thick sour cream
- ¼ cup honey
- 2 tbsp. sugar
- 6 egg yolks, beaten
- ⅛ tsp. salt
- 7 egg whites

Blend the cheese with the sour cream until quite smooth. Add honey, sugar, egg yolks, and salt. Beat thoroughly for 5 minutes. If possible, use an electric mixer at a slow speed. Preheat oven to moderate, 325°F.

Beat the egg whites until stiff but not dry. Fold them into the cheese mixture carefully and pour into a buttered 2-quart soufflé dish. Bake 45 minutes.

Serve at once.

Serve with Strawberry Sauce, see page 229.

Robert's Cream-Cheese Soufflé

[4 to 6 servings]

5 egg yolks, beaten
½ cup powdered sugar
1 pound cream cheese
1 tbsp. sifted all-purpose flour
¼ cup heavy cream
2 tbsp. butter, melted
3 tbsp. chopped candied fruit
4 tbsp. graham-cracker crumbs
5 egg whites

Beat the egg yolks and sugar together thoroughly. Force the cream cheese through a sieve. Add to the yolks. Beat thoroughly. If possible use an electric mixer. Add the flour, cream, butter, and candied fruit as you beat.

Preheat oven to moderate, 325°F. Butter a 1½-quart soufflé dish, and dust with 3 tablespoons of the graham-cracker crumbs.

Beat the egg whites until stiff but not dry. Fold them into the cheese mixture carefully. Pour the soufflé mixture into the dish. Sprinkle the remaining 1 tablespoon of crumbs over the top. Bake 50 minutes.

Serve at once.

Cream-Puff Soufflé

[4 servings]

1 cup sifted confectioners' sugar
½ cup sifted all-purpose flour
1 cup milk
2 tsp. almond extract
⅛ tsp. salt
3 egg yolks
5 egg whites
2 tbsp. sliced blanched almonds

Sift sugar and flour together into a saucepan. Add milk gradually, with almond extract and salt. Mix well, and place over very low heat. Cook, stirring constantly with a wire whisk, until boiling point is reached. The mixture will thicken very suddenly, so do not stop stirring even momentarily.

Beat the egg yolks in a bowl until light colored. Add the hot mixture very slowly, beating constantly to prevent curdling. Let cool for 15 minutes.

Preheat oven to moderate, 350°F. Butter a 1½-quart soufflé dish and dust with confectioners' sugar.

Beat the egg whites until stiff but not dry. Fold the whites into the almond mixture.

Pour the soufflé into the dish. Sprinkle almonds on top. Place in a shallow pan of hot water. Bake 35 minutes.

Serve at once.

Serve with Chocolate Sauce, see page 225.

Crème de Cacao Soufflé

[4 servings]

- 2 tbsp. butter
- 2 tbsp. sifted all-purpose flour
- ⅔ cup milk, scalded
- 1 square (1 oz.) unsweetened chocolate
- ¼ cup sugar
- ¼ cup crème de cacao cordial
- 3 egg yolks, beaten
- 4 egg whites

Melt butter in a saucepan, add flour, and stir until smooth. Add the scalded milk gradually, stirring constantly. Cook until thick and smooth, about 5 minutes, stirring occasionally.

Place chocolate, sugar, and crème de cacao in a small saucepan over very low heat. Stir until the chocolate and sugar melt, and the mixture is smooth. Add to the milk sauce, stir well. Let cool for 15 minutes. And the egg yolks, and mix.

Preheat oven to moderate, 350°F. Butter a 1½-quart soufflé dish, and dust with sugar.

Beat the egg whites until stiff but not dry. Fold them into the chocolate mixture carefully. Pour the soufflé into the dish and sprinkle a little sugar on top. Bake 45 minutes.

Serve at once.

Date-and-Nut Soufflé

[4 servings]

¼ cup sugar
¼ cup water
1 cup chopped pitted dates
½ cup chopped pecans
1 tsp. lemon juice
½ tsp. grated lemon rind
2 tbsp. ground pecans
4 egg whites

Combine the sugar and water in a saucepan. Heat, stirring occasionally, until the sugar is dissolved. Add dates, bring to boiling point, and boil 1 minute. Add chopped pecans, lemon juice and rind, and stir. Remove from the heat, and set aside to cool for 15 minutes.

Preheat oven to moderate, 325°F. Butter a 1½-quart soufflé dish, and dust with 1 tablespoon of the ground pecans.

Beat the egg whites until stiff but not dry. Fold them into the date mixture carefully. Pour into the dish, and sprinkle the remaining tablespoon of pecans on top. Place in a shallow pan of hot water. Bake 40 minutes.

Serve at once.

This is a rich soufflé, and is best served after a rather light entrée.

Fresh-Fig Soufflé

[4 servings]

- 2 tbsp. butter
- ¼ cup sifted all-purpose flour
- 1 cup milk, scalded
- 3 egg yolks
- ¼ cup sugar
- 2 tbsp. brandy
- 12 fresh figs, washed and chopped
- 4 egg whites

Melt the butter in a saucepan, add flour, and stir until smooth over low heat. Stir in milk gradually. Continue cooking until thick, about 5 minutes, stirring frequently. Remove from heat, and let cool for 10 minutes. Beat the egg yolks until light in color. Gradually add to the white sauce, beating constantly to prevent curdling. Add sugar, brandy, and figs, and stir well together. Let cool for 5 minutes.

Preheat oven to moderate, 325°F. Butter a 1½-quart soufflé dish, and sprinkle with sugar.

Beat the egg whites until stiff but not dry. Fold them into the fig mixture carefully. Pour into the dish. Bake 45 minutes.

Serve at once.

Serve with whipped cream, with or without brandy flavor.

Canned-Fig Soufflé

[3 to 4 servings]

1 cup canned yellow figs
3 tbsp. sugar
2 tbsp. brandy
5 tbsp. ground pecans
4 egg whites
1 tsp. orange juice

Drain the figs, and force them through a sieve. Heat in a saucepan, and add 2 tablespoons of sugar and the brandy. Stir well, and set aside to cool for 15 minutes.

Preheat oven to moderate, 325°F. Butter a 1-quart soufflé dish very well, and dust with finely ground pecans.

Beat the egg whites until stiff but not dry. Add to them the remaining 1 tablespoon of sugar, and the orange juice. Mix and fold into the fig mixture carefully.

Pour the soufflé into the dish, and set in a shallow pan of water. Bake 30 minutes.

Serve at once.

May be served with plain, or Brandied Whipped Cream, see page 230.

Fruit-Compote Soufflé

[6 servings]

- 3 peaches
- 2 pears
- 10 cherries
- ½ cup seedless grapes
- 5 tbsp. sugar
- 3 tbsp. butter
- ½ cup crumbled vanilla wafers
- ⅔ cup light cream, scalded
- ½ tsp. vanilla extract
- 1 tbsp. brandy
- 3 egg yolks, beaten
- 3 egg whites

Wash and drain the fruit; peel the peaches and pears, and cut into small pieces. Pit the cherries; stem the grapes, and mix all together in an enamel or glass saucepan. Add 4 tablespoons of the sugar. Cook over low heat 10 minutes, stirring occasionally. Set aside to cool for 15 minutes.

Melt the butter in another saucepan; add cooky crumbs and cook 3 minutes over low heat, stirring well. Stir cream in; add the remaining 1 tablespoon of sugar, the vanilla, and brandy. Let cool for 10 minutes. Add the egg yolks gradually, beating steadily. Let cool again for 5 minutes.

Preheat oven to moderate, 350°F. Butter a 1½-quart soufflé dish, and sprinkle with sugar. Place the cooked fruit on the bottom of the dish.

Beat the egg whites until stiff but not dry. Fold them into the yolk mixture carefully. Pour on top of the fruit mixture in the soufflé dish. Bake 35 minutes.

Serve at once.

Ginger Soufflé

[4 to 6 servings]

2 tbsp. butter
2 tbsp. sifted all-purpose flour
½ cup sugar
1 cup light cream
⅛ tsp. salt
¼ tsp. powdered ginger
6 egg yolks
2 tbsp. brandy
1 cup ground preserved ginger
1 tbsp. confectioners' sugar
6 egg whites

Melt the butter in a saucepan; stir flour in until smooth, add sugar, cream, salt, and powdered ginger, and cook over low heat until thick and smooth, about 5 minutes, stirring constantly. Remove from heat and let cool for 10 minutes. Beat the egg yolks in a bowl until light in color. Add the cream mixture gradually, beating constantly to prevent curdling. Let cool for 5 minutes. Add the brandy and the preserved ginger and stir well.

Preheat oven to moderate, 350°F. Butter a 2-quart soufflé dish carefully, and dust it with half of the confectioners' sugar.

Beat the egg whites until stiff but not dry. Fold them into the yolk mixture carefully. Pour into soufflé dish. Sprinkle remaining sugar on top. Bake 25 minutes.

Serve at once.

Serve with sweetened whipped cream.

Ginger-and-Candied-Fruit Soufflé

[4 servings]

2 tbsp. butter
3/8 cup sifted all-purpose flour
1 cup light cream
1/4 cup sugar
3 egg yolks, beaten
2 tbsp. chopped candied fruit
2 tbsp. chopped preserved ginger
1 tsp. powdered ginger
dash salt
3 egg whites
2 tbsp. ground pecans

Melt the butter in the upper part of double boiler. Blend in flour. Add cream and sugar gradually, stirring constantly. Place over hot water and cook until thick and smooth, about 5 minutes. Let cool 5 minutes. Add the egg yolks, beating very well; add fruit, ginger, powdered ginger, and salt. Mix well.

Preheat oven to moderate, 325°F. Butter four 1½-cup soufflé dishes and dust with the pecans.

Beat the egg whites until stiff but not dry. Fold them into the ginger mixture. Pour into the soufflé dishes. Bake 25 minutes.

Serve at once.

Serve with Ginger Sauce, see page 227.

Guava Soufflé

[4 servings]

- 3 tbsp. butter
- 3 tbsp. sifted all-purpose flour
- 2 tbsp. sugar
- 1¼ cups light cream, scalded
- 4 egg yolks
- 1¼ cups canned guava shells *or* ½ cup guava jelly
- 1 tbsp. brandy
- 2 tbsp. ground almonds
- 4 egg whites

Melt the butter in a saucepan, add the flour and sugar, and stir until smooth. Add the cream gradually, stirring constantly until the boiling point is reached. Cook until thick and smooth, stirring occasionally, about 5 minutes. Let cool for 5 minutes. Beat the egg yolks until light in color. Add the cream sauce gradually to the yolks, stirring constantly to prevent curdling. Let cool for 5 minutes.

If you are using canned guava shells, drain them, and force through a sieve. Guava jelly also must be forced through a sieve. Add the guava to the yolk mixture; add the brandy and mix well.

Preheat oven to moderate, 350°F. Butter a 1½-quart soufflé dish, and dust with some of the almonds.

Beat the egg whites until stiff but not dry. Fold them into the guava mixture carefully. Pour mixture into the dish, and sprinkle the remaining almonds on top. Bake 35 minutes.

Serve at once.

Gooseberry Soufflé

[4 to 6 servings]

¼ cup brown sugar (packed)
¼ cup water
1 cup gooseberries
6 egg yolks
¼ cup granulated sugar
1 tsp. vanilla extract
¾ cup heavy cream
6 egg whites
2 tbsp. sifted all-purpose flour

Combine the brown sugar and water in a saucepan, bring to boiling and boil until syrupy, about 5 minutes. Add gooseberries, and cook 5 minutes; spoon the syrup over the gooseberries a few times while cooking. Drain. Set aside.

Beat the egg yolks in the upper part of a double boiler until light in color; add granulated sugar and vanilla. Continue beating until the eggs become fluffy, about 3 minutes. Add the cream gradually, mixing well. Place over hot water and cook until thick, about 5 minutes, stirring constantly. Add the gooseberry mixture, stir well, and set aside to cool for 10 minutes.

Preheat oven to moderate, 325°F. Butter a 2-quart soufflé dish, and dust with sugar.

Place the egg whites in a bowl, and sprinkle flour on top. Beat until stiff. Fold into the berry mixture carefully. Pour into soufflé dish, and sprinkle sugar on top. Bake 35 minutes.

Serve at once.

Grenoble Soufflé

[4 servings]

¼ cup butter
¼ cup sifted all-purpose flour
1 cup light cream
2 tbsp. brandy
1 tbsp. orange juice
⅛ tsp. almond extract
4 egg yolks
½ cup sugar
1 tsp. grated lemon rind
dash salt
½ cup chopped walnuts
3 tbsp. ground walnuts
4 egg whites

Melt the butter in the top of a double boiler, stir in the flour, and stir and cook until mixture bubbles. Add cream, and continue cooking until thick and smooth, about 5 minutes, stirring constantly. Remove from heat, let cool. Add the brandy, orange juice, and almond extract gradually, mixing well. Beat the egg yolks in a bowl until light in color, add sugar, lemon rind, salt, and chopped walnuts, and mix well. Combine with the cream mixture, beating constantly.

Preheat oven to moderate, 350°F. Butter a 1½-quart soufflé dish, and dust with 2 tablespoons of the ground walnuts.

Beat the egg whites until stiff but not dry. Fold them into the yolk mixture carefully. Pour soufflé into the dish, and sprinkle the remaining walnuts on top. Bake 30 minutes.

Serve at once.

Hazelnut Soufflé

[4 servings]

4 egg yolks
¼ cup sugar
3 tbsp. sifted all-purpose flour
1 tbsp. brandy
¼ tsp. salt
1 cup heavy cream
¾ cup ground hazelnuts (filberts)
3 tbsp. butter
4 egg whites

Beat the egg yolks in a bowl; add sugar and flour gradually; beat until creamy. Add the brandy and salt; mix well.

Heat the cream and nuts together in a saucepan, until bubbles begin to form on the sides of the pan. Add the yolk mixture, stirring continuously. Cook over low heat until the mixture thickens, about 5 minutes, stirring constantly. Add butter, mix well and let cool for 15 minutes. Preheat oven to moderate, 325°F.

Beat the egg whites until stiff but not dry. Fold them into the nut mixture carefully. Pour into a buttered 1½-quart soufflé dish. Bake 30 minutes.

Serve at once.

This dish may be accompanied by Brandied Whipped Cream, see page 238.

Although it will fall a little, the soufflé may be served cold, especially if topped with some of the brandied whipped cream.

Honey Soufflé

[4 servings]

4 egg yolks
1 tbsp. sifted all-purpose flour
¼ tsp. salt
dash nutmeg
¾ cup powdered sugar
2 tbsp. brandy
½ cup honey
½ cup butter, melted
5 egg whites
1 tbsp. ground walnuts

Beat the egg yolks in a bowl until light in color. Sift flour, salt, nutmeg, and sugar together into the yolks. Stir until well mixed and smooth in consistency. Add the brandy and stir well. Mix honey and butter, and add gradually to the egg mixture, beating smoothly. Preheat oven to moderate, 350°F.

Beat the egg whites until stiff but not dry. Fold them into the honey mixture carefully.

Pour into an unbuttered 1½-quart soufflé dish, and sprinkle the walnuts on top. Place dish in a shallow pan of hot water. Bake 40 minutes.

Serve at once.

This soufflé is particularly good when served with whipped cream.

Java Soufflé

[4 servings]

3 tbsp. butter
3 tbsp. sifted all-purpose flour
¾ cup brewed double-strength tea
⅓ cup sugar
4 egg yolks
¼ cup chopped pistachio nuts
4 egg whites

Melt the butter in a saucepan, add the flour, and stir well until smooth. Add the tea gradually, stirring constantly. Add sugar, and cook over low heat for 5 minutes, stirring. Let cool for 5 minutes.

Beat the egg yolks in a bowl until light in color; gradually add the tea mixture to the yolks, beating steadily to prevent curdling. Add 2 tablespoons of the chopped nuts, and mix well. Let cool for 5 minutes.

Preheat oven to moderate, 350°F. Butter a 1½-quart soufflé dish and dust with sugar.

Beat the egg whites until stiff but not dry. Fold them into the tea mixture carefully. Pour the soufflé into the dish, and sprinkle the remaining nuts on top. Bake 35 minutes.

Serve at once.

Jelly Soufflé

[2 to 4 servings]

¼ cup jelly
½ cup ground walnuts
4 egg whites

Melt the jelly in a saucepan over low heat. Add nuts. Let cool 10 minutes. Preheat oven to moderate, 350°F. Butter a 1-quart soufflé dish.

Beat the egg whites until stiff but not dry. Fold into the jelly and nuts. Pour into the soufflé dish. Set the dish in a shallow pan of hot water. Bake 25 minutes.

Serve at once.

Lemon Soufflé

[2 or 3 servings]

4 egg yolks
¾ cup sugar
¼ cup lemon juice
1 tbsp. grated lemon rind
¼ tsp. salt
4 egg whites

Beat the egg yolks in a bowl until thick and frothy. Add sugar gradually, beating well. Add lemon juice and rind, and mix well.

Preheat oven to moderate, 350°F. Butter a 1-quart soufflé dish and dust with sugar.

Sprinkle salt on the egg whites, and beat until stiff, but not dry. Fold the egg whites into the lemon mixture carefully. Pour soufflé into the dish. Place in a shallow pan of hot water. Bake 35 minutes.

Serve at once.

Lemon-Rind Soufflé

[2 to 4 servings]

4 egg whites
¼ cup sugar
1 tsp. vanilla extract
½ tsp. lemon extract
2 tbsp. grated lemon rind

Beat the egg whites until stiff but not dry. Add sugar slowly and carefully, beating lightly. Add vanilla and lemon extract, and all of the lemon rind but ½ tablespoon. Stir together.

Butter the top of a 1½-quart double boiler carefully. Sprinkle with the remaining ½ tablespoon of lemon rind. Pour the mixture in and *cover*. Place over, but not touching, hot water, and cook 50 minutes. When ready, run a knife carefully around the edge, tap the sides gently, and unmold carefully onto a warm plate.

Serve at once.

Serve with Lemon Sauce, see page 227.

Meringue Soufflé

[6 servings]

- 2 egg yolks
- ¼ cup powdered sugar
- 1 cup milk
- 1 tsp. vanilla extract
- 6 slices pound cake (cut half-inch thick)
- 2 tbsp. raspberry jelly or jam

Beat the egg yolks in a bowl, add the sugar gradually. Add milk and vanilla, stirring well. Pour over pound cake in a bowl. Let soak for 10 minutes. Remove the slices very carefully and place on a buttered cooky sheet. Reserve the liquid. Spread 1 teaspoon of raspberry jelly or jam over each slice of cake.

To prepare the soufflé mixture use:

- 4 egg whites
- dash salt
- 1 cup powdered sugar
- 3 tbsp. reserved egg-and-milk mixture
- ½ tsp. vanilla extract

Preheat oven to low, 275°F.

Beat the egg whites until stiff but not dry. Add salt and sugar gradually, and continue beating for 1 minute. Place in the top of a double boiler over hot water, add the reserved egg-and-milk mixture and vanilla. Cook until well blended, about 5 minutes; stir only enough to mix.

Spoon this mixture over the prepared cake, forming the highest possible mounds on each slice. Bake 40 minutes.

Transfer to warmed plates.

Serve at once.

Molasses Soufflé

[4 servings]

4 tbsp. butter
¼ cup sifted all-purpose flour
½ cup milk, scalded
¼ cup heavy cream, scalded
½ cup molasses
¼ tsp. powdered cinnamon
dash salt
¼ tsp. powdered ginger
3 egg yolks
3 tbsp. brown sugar
4 egg whites

Melt the butter in a saucepan; stir in the flour until smooth. Add the milk and cream slowly, stirring constantly. Bring to a boil. Add molasses, cinnamon, salt, and ginger. Mix well. Cook over low heat 5 minutes, stirring occasionally. Set aside to cool. Beat the egg yolks in a bowl until light; add sugar, creaming until thick. Add the molasses mixture slowly to the yolks, stirring constantly to prevent curdling. Preheat oven to moderate, 325°F.

Beat the egg whites until stiff but not dry. Fold them into the molasses mixture carefully. Pour into a buttered 1½-quart soufflé dish. Bake 45 minutes.

Serve at once.

Whip 1 cup heavy cream, add ½ teaspoon powdered ginger; serve with the soufflé.

Orange Soufflé

[4 servings]

4 egg yolks
¾ cup sugar
¼ tsp. salt
¼ cup orange juice
1 tbsp. grated orange rind
½ tsp. orange extract
3 drops orange pure-food coloring (optional)
4 egg whites

Beat the yolks in a bowl; add sugar and salt, beating well until well creamed. Add orange juice, rind, extract, and coloring. Mix well together.

Preheat oven to moderate, 350°F. Butter a 1½-quart soufflé dish, and dust with sugar.

Beat the egg whites until stiff but not dry. Fold carefully into the orange mixture. Pour into the soufflé dish. Sprinkle sugar on top. Bake 30 minutes.

Serve at once.

Orange Liqueur Soufflé

[4 servings]

- ⅜ cup sugar
- ¾ cup orange juice
- 3 tbsp. grated orange rind
- 2 tbsp. grated lemon rind
- 4 egg yolks
- 3 tbsp. curaçao, Triple Sec, *or* Grand Marnier
- 4 egg whites

Combine the sugar and orange juice in an enamel or glass saucepan, and bring to a boil. Continue cooking over low heat for 10 minutes, stirring frequently. Add orange and lemon rind, and stir. Set aside to cool for 10 minutes. Beat the egg yolks in a bowl until light in color. Pour the orange mixture into the yolks gradually, stirring steadily to prevent curdling. Add the liqueur, and stir. Let cool for 10 minutes more.

Preheat oven to moderate, 350°F. Butter a 1½-quart soufflé dish, and sprinkle it with sugar.

Beat the egg whites until stiff but not dry. Fold them into the liqueur mixture carefully. Pour into the soufflé dish and sprinkle a little sugar on top. Bake 30 minutes.

Serve at once.

Orange-Marmalade Soufflé

[2 or 3 servings]

4 egg whites
¼ tsp. cream of tartar
2 tbsp. sugar
3 tbsp. orange marmalade
½ tsp. vanilla extract

Beat the egg whites with cream of tartar until stiff but not dry. Add sugar gradually, beating well. Fold in the marmalade slowly and carefully; add vanilla, stirring gently.

Butter the top of a 1-quart double boiler. Pour the soufflé mixture into it, and place over, but not touching, hot water. *Cover.* Cook over high heat 45 minutes. When ready, run a knife carefully around the edge of the soufflé, tap the sides of the pan gently, and unmold soufflé onto a warmed plate.

Serve at once.

Orange-Pecan Soufflé

[4 servings]

3 tbsp. butter
3 tbsp. sifted all-purpose flour
¾ cup milk, scalded
¼ cup sugar
dash salt
4 egg yolks
¼ cup orange juice
2 tsp. grated orange rind
5 egg whites
3 tbsp. ground pecans
3 tbsp. fruit brandy (cherry, apricot, etc.)
6 ladyfingers, halved

Melt the butter in a saucepan, stir the flour in until smooth. Add the milk gradually, stirring constantly. Add sugar and salt, and cook over low heat 5 minutes, stirring constantly. Beat the egg yolks in a bowl until light in color. Add the hot milk mixture gradually, stirring constantly to prevent curdling. Divide the resulting yolk mixture in half, by pouring as evenly as possible into 2 separate bowls. Set aside to cool for 15 minutes.

To one bowl, add the orange juice and rind, and mix together. Preheat oven to moderate, 350°F. Butter a 1½-quart soufflé dish, and sprinkle with sugar.

Beat the egg whites until stiff but not dry. Fold half of the whites into the orange mixture carefully.

To the other bowl add the pecans, and stir well. Fold in the remaining half of the beaten whites carefully. Pour the pecan mixture into the soufflé dish. Sprinkle the brandy over ladyfingers, and place them over the pecan mixture. Pour the orange mixture on top. Bake 35 minutes.

Serve at once.

Hot-and-Cold Soufflé

[6 servings]

6 very large oranges, *or* 6 small grapefruit
1 pint orange sherbet
2 egg yolks
¼ tsp. vanilla extract
3 egg whites
½ cup sugar

Wash the oranges or grapefruit. Cut ¼ off the top of each. With sharp knife remove the pulp and juice carefully, leaving the shells intact. Place shells in the coldest part of the refrigerator (or in a deep freeze) for 1 hour. Remove, and fill each to the top with firm sherbet, packing it down as hard as possible so that no air spaces remain. Return them to the refrigerator or deep freeze. Preheat oven to very hot, 475°F.

Beat the egg yolks in a bowl until light in color. Add the vanilla and stir. Beat the egg whites until stiff. Add the sugar by the spoonful, beating constantly. Fold into the yolks gently.

Remove the filled fruit shells from the refrigerator. Spoon the soufflé mixture thickly on top of each, covering the edges. Place on a buttered baking sheet, and bake 5 minutes.

Serve at once.

Do not delay in serving, because although the shells will insulate the sherbet, it will not keep too long.

Parisienne Soufflé

[4 to 6 servings]

2 tbsp. butter
2 tbsp. sifted all-purpose flour
½ cup sugar
1 cup light cream, scalded
5 egg yolks, beaten
3 tbsp. Triple Sec *or* Cointreau
dash salt
5 egg whites
8 ladyfingers
1 tbsp. confectioners' sugar
¼ cup plum *or* raspberry jam, softened by heating 5 minutes

Cream the butter and flour in a saucepan until smooth. Add sugar and cream, mixing well. Cook 5 minutes, stirring occasionally. Remove from the heat, and add the egg yolks slowly, beating continuously. Add the Triple Sec or Cointreau, and salt. Mix again. Let cool for 15 minutes.

Preheat oven to moderate, 375°F. Butter a 1½-quart soufflé dish. Line with ladyfingers. Sprinkle sugar in the bottom of the dish.

Beat the egg whites until stiff but not dry. Fold into yolk mixture carefully. Pour half of the soufflé mixture into the dish. Pour jam on top, add the remaining soufflé mixture. Bake 25 minutes.

Serve at once.

Serve with whipped cream.

Peach Soufflé

[4 servings]

8 large peaches
½ cup water
3 tbsp. lemon juice
¼ cup Grand Marnier *or* Curaçao
2 tbsp. grated orange rind
dash salt
¼ cup sugar
¼ tsp. almond extract
3 egg yolks, beaten
4 egg whites

Wash, peel and slice the peaches; cook them in the water 10 minutes. Force through a sieve. Let cool for 10 minutes. Combine the peach pulp with the lemon juice, add the Grand Marnier or curaçao and mix well. Add orange rind, salt, and sugar. Bring to a boil over low heat; remove and let cool for 5 minutes. Add almond extract and the egg yolks, beating continuously.

Preheat oven to moderate, 375°F. Butter a 1½-quart soufflé dish, and dust with sugar.

Beat the egg whites until stiff but not dry. Fold them into the peach mixture carefully. Pour into the soufflé dish, and sprinkle a little sugar on top. Place in a shallow pan of hot water. Bake 30 minutes.

Serve at once.

Peach-and-Almond Soufflé

[4 servings]

1½ cups sliced canned peaches
3 tbsp. cherry brandy
4 egg whites
1 cup powdered sugar
¾ cup ground blanched almonds

Drain the peaches. Pour the cherry brandy on the fruit, and let marinate 20 minutes.

Preheat oven to moderate, 375°F. Butter a 1-quart soufflé dish carefully, and sprinkle with sugar. Arrange the peaches in the bottom and around the sides of the dish.

Beat the egg whites until stiff. Add sugar, 1 tablespoon at a time, beating steadily. Fold in almonds.

Pour the almond soufflé mixture onto the peaches. Place the dish in a shallow pan of hot water. Bake 35 minutes.

Serve at once.

Pecan Soufflé

[4 to 6 servings]

6 egg yolks
½ cup sugar
1 tsp. vanilla extract
⅔ cup ground pecans
2 tbsp. brandy
6 ladyfingers
⅛ tsp. salt
6 egg whites

Beat the egg yolks in a bowl until light in color. Sift the sugar, and add to the yolks gradually, beating steadily until the mixture is creamy. Add vanilla, pecans, and brandy, and stir well.

Preheat oven to moderate, 325°F. Butter a 1-quart soufflé dish, and line the bottom and sides with ladyfingers.

Sprinkle the salt on the egg whites and beat until stiff but not dry. Fold them into the nut mixture carefully. Pour the mixture into the soufflé dish. Bake 40 minutes.

Serve at once.

Serve with whipped cream.

Pineapple-Meringue Soufflé

[4 servings]

½ cup butter
⅔ cup sugar
4 egg yolks
5 tbsp. grated almonds
1 cup canned crushed pineapple, drained
1 tbsp. lemon juice
4 egg whites
⅛ tsp. salt

Cream the butter in a bowl until smooth, add sugar gradually, mixing until creamy. Beat the egg yolks until light in color; combine with the sugar mixture, beating well. Add almonds, pineapple, and lemon juice, and mix well. Preheat oven to moderate, 325°F.

Beat the egg whites with the salt until stiff but not dry. Fold carefully into the pineapple mixture. Pour into a buttered 2-quart soufflé dish. Now prepare as quickly as possible:

2 egg whites
¼ tsp. salt
¼ cup sugar
1 tsp. vanilla extract

Beat the egg whites and salt until stiff. Gradually add the sugar, and continue beating. Add vanilla and fold it in gently. Pile this mixture on top of the soufflé. Bake 30 minutes.

Serve at once.

Prune-Custard Soufflé

[4 servings]

- 4 egg yolks
- ½ cup sugar
- 1 cup light cream
- 6 tbsp. butter
- 1 tsp. lemon rind
- 1 tbsp. brandy
- ½ tsp. vanilla extract
- 4 egg whites
- 1 cup chopped and pitted cooked prunes
- ¼ cup sliced blanched almonds

Beat the egg yolks in the top of a double boiler. Add sugar, and continue beating until light and frothy. Gradually add cream and butter. Set the pan over hot water and cook, stirring constantly until the mixture is thick and smooth. Add lemon rind, brandy, and vanilla. Set aside to cool for 15 minutes.

Preheat oven to moderate, 350°F. Butter a 1½-quart soufflé dish carefully, and dust with sugar. Arrange the prunes on the bottom of the dish. Sprinkle all of the almonds but 1 tablespoon on top of the prunes.

Beat the egg whites until stiff but not dry. Fold them into the yolk mixture carefully. Pour into the soufflé dish on top of prunes and almonds. Sprinkle the reserved tablespoon of almonds on top. Bake 35 minutes.

Serve at once.

Prune-and-Nut Soufflé

[4 servings]

1 pound prunes
1 cup water
5 tbsp. sugar
1 tsp. lemon juice
1 tsp. grated lemon rind
½ cup chopped walnuts
5 egg whites

Cook the prunes in the water until tender, about 20 minutes. Drain, and pit the prunes. Grind the fruit, which should result in about 1 cup of prune pulp. Add sugar, lemon juice, and rind to the prune pulp. Add nuts, and mix all together very well.

Preheat oven to moderate, 350°F. Butter a 1½-quart soufflé dish, and dust with sugar.

Beat the egg whites until stiff but not dry. Fold them into the prune mixture carefully. Pour into the soufflé dish; dust the top with a little sugar. Place in a shallow pan of hot water. Bake 35 minutes.

Serve at once.

This soufflé is often served with whipped cream flavored with a little vanilla.

Pumpkin Soufflé

[4 servings]

- 2 cups canned pumpkin
- ¼ cup brown sugar (packed)
- 2 tbsp. dark corn syrup
- ½ tsp. salt
- ¼ tsp. powdered mace (optional)
- 1 tsp. powdered ginger
- 2 tbsp. grated orange rind
- 1 cup light cream
- 3 egg yolks, beaten
- 3 egg whites

Force the pumpkin through a strainer; add sugar, corn syrup, salt, mace, ginger, and orange rind. Mix well together. Add the cream and the egg yolks, stirring steadily.

Preheat oven to moderate, 350°F. Butter a 1½-quart soufflé dish, and dust lightly with flour.

Beat the egg whites until stiff but not dry. Fold them into the pumpkin mixture carefully. Pour into the dish. Bake 50 minutes.

Serve at once.

Raspberry Soufflé

[4 servings]

- 4 egg yolks
- ½ cup sugar
- ¼ cup sifted all-purpose flour
- 1½ cups milk, scalded
- 1 tsp. vanilla extract
- 1 cup sliced raspberries, fresh or frozen
- 1 tbsp. powdered sugar
- 2 tbsp. fruit brandy (cherry, apricot, etc.)
- 5 egg whites

Beat the egg yolks in a saucepan, add sugar, beating well until light and creamy. Add flour, and mix until blended. Add milk gradually, stirring well. Cook over low heat, stirring constantly, until boiling point is reached. Remove from the heat immediately. Add vanilla and stir well. Let cool; strain.

Sprinkle the berries with the powdered sugar and brandy. Add to the custard mixture. Mix well.

Preheat oven to moderate, 325°F. Butter a 1½-quart soufflé dish, and sprinkle with sugar.

Beat the egg whites until stiff but not dry. Fold them into the fruit mixture. Pour into the dish, and sprinkle a little sugar and any remaining berries on top. Bake 35 minutes.

Serve at once.

Rice-Ring Soufflé

[4 to 6 servings]

¾ cup rice, uncooked
1 cup water
2 cups milk, scalded
½ cup sugar
2 tbsp. butter
½ tsp. salt
1 tsp. vanilla extract
5 egg yolks, beaten
5 egg whites

Wash the rice thoroughly; drain; combine with the 1 cup of water and bring to a boil. Remove from the heat and let soak 5 minutes. Drain, and wash again, to remove excess starch. Return to saucepan, add milk, sugar, butter, and salt. Cover, and cook over low heat 30 minutes. Drain well. Let cool for 10 minutes. Add vanilla and the egg yolks, mixing carefully.

Preheat oven to moderate, 350°F. Butter an 8-inch ring mold and dust with sugar.

Beat the egg whites until stiff but not dry. Fold them into rice mixture carefully. Pour soufflé into the mold. Place mold in a shallow pan of hot water, and bake 45 minutes. Allow to settle for a few minutes, run a knife around the edge of the pan and then turn soufflé out onto a warmed platter.

Serve at once.

Serve with Brown-Sugar Sauce, see page 224.

Sauterne Soufflé

[4 servings]

3 tbsp. butter
2 tbsp. sifted all-purpose flour
1 cup sauterne
½ cup sugar
1 tsp. grated lemon rind
2 tbsp. brandy
4 egg yolks, beaten
2 tbsp. finely chopped candied fruit
dash salt
4 egg whites

Melt the butter in a saucepan, add flour, and stir until smooth. Add wine gradually, stirring constantly. Add sugar and lemon rind, and cook over low heat until thick and smooth, about 5 minutes, stirring occasionally. Let cool for 10 minutes. Add brandy, the egg yolks, and candied fruit, and mix all together well.

Preheat oven to moderate, 350°F. Butter a 1½-quart soufflé dish, and sprinkle with sugar.

Sprinkle the salt on the egg whites, and beat them until stiff but not dry. Fold into the yolk mixture. Pour into the dish, and sprinkle a little sugar on top. Bake 35 minutes.

Serve at once.

Sherry-Lemon Soufflé

[4 servings]

- 2 tbsp. sifted all-purpose flour
- ½ cup sugar
- ½ cup milk
- ½ cup sherry
- 3 egg yolks
- 1 tbsp. grated lemon rind
- 3 tbsp. lemon juice
- ¼ tsp. salt
- 3 egg whites

Combine the flour and sugar in a saucepan. Add the milk and sherry gradually. Cook over low heat, stirring constantly, until smooth and thick, about 5 minutes. Remove from the heat.

Beat the egg yolks with the lemon rind and juice until light. Add the milk mixture, stirring well. Let cool for 10 minutes.

Preheat oven to moderate, 350°F. Butter a 1½-quart soufflé dish and dust with sugar.

Sprinkle the salt on the egg whites, and beat until stiff but not dry. Fold into yolk mixture carefully. Pour into soufflé dish. Bake 30 minutes.

Serve at once.

Serve with Brown-Sugar Sauce, see page 224.

Soufflé a la Russe

[4 to 6 servings]

- 6 egg yolks
- 1½ cups powdered sugar
- 3 tbsp. cherry brandy
- ¼ tsp. salt
- ½ tsp. almond extract
- ¼ cup crumbled ladyfingers
- 2 tbsp. ground blanched almonds
- 6 egg whites

Beat the egg yolks in a bowl until light and fluffy. Add sugar gradually, and beat until smooth. Add cherry brandy, salt, and almond extract. Mix well for at least 1 minute. Fold in ladyfinger crumbs, but reserve 1 tablespoon.

Preheat oven to moderate, 350°F. Butter a 2-quart soufflé dish, and dust with the ground almonds.

Beat the egg whites until stiff but not dry. Fold them into the crumb mixture carefully. Pour into the dish, and sprinkle the top with the reserved tablespoon of ladyfinger crumbs. Bake 30 minutes.

Serve at once.

Strawberry Soufflé

[4 servings]

- ⅜ cup sifted all-purpose flour
- 5 tbsp. sugar
- ¼ tsp. salt
- ¾ cup light cream
- 2 tbsp. butter
- 1 cup mashed strawberries, fresh or frozen
- 2 tbsp. brandy
- 1 tbsp. orange juice
- 3 egg yolks, beaten
- ½ cup sliced strawberries, fresh or frozen
- 4 egg whites

Combine flour, sugar, salt, and cream in a saucepan. Cook over low heat, stirring constantly until the mixture is smooth and thick, about 5 minutes. Add butter, mashed strawberries, brandy, and orange juice, and stir. Remove from the heat, and let cool for 15 minutes. Add the egg yolks gradually, stirring constantly. Add all but 2 tablespoons of the sliced strawberries.

Perheat oven to moderate, 375°F. Butter a 1½-quart soufflé dish, and sprinkle lightly with sugar.

Beat the egg whites until stiff but not dry. Fold them into the fruit mixture carefully. Pour into the dish. Decorate the top with the 2 tablespoons of reserved sliced strawberries. Place dish in a shallow pan of hot water. Bake 35 minutes.

Serve at once.

This soufflé may be served with whipped cream, or Vanilla Sauce, see page 229.

Walnut Soufflé

[4 servings]

- ⅜ cup powdered sugar
- ½ cup water
- ⅛ tsp. powdered cinnamon
- ⅛ tsp. grated nutmeg
- ¾ cup ground walnuts
- 1 tbsp. zwieback crumbs
- 2 tsp. grated orange rind
- 5 egg yolks
- 5 egg whites

Combine the sugar, water, cinnamon, and nutmeg in a saucepan. Place over low heat and bring to a boil, stirring steadily. Continue cooking and stirring until mixture thickens, about 10 minutes. Add all but 1 tablespoon of walnuts, the crumbs, and orange rind and mix all together well. Remove from the heat. Beat the egg yolks in a bowl; add the hot mixture gradually to the yolks, stirring constantly. Let cool for 5 minutes.

Preheat oven to moderate, 350°F. Butter a 1½-quart soufflé dish.

Beat the egg whites until stiff but not dry. Fold them into the nut mixture carefully. Pour into the soufflé dish. Sprinkle remaining walnuts over the top of the soufflé. Bake 30 minutes.

Serve at once.

Walnut-and-Butterscotch Soufflé

[4 to 6 servings]

⅔ cup brown sugar (packed)
½ cup confectioners' sugar
6 egg yolks
1 tsp. vanilla extract
⅔ cup ground walnuts
⅛ tsp. salt
6 egg whites

Sift the two kinds of sugar together. (It is important that confectioners' sugar be used; granulated sugar should not be substituted.) Beat the egg yolks until light in color. Add sugar gradually, and continue beating until creamy. Add vanilla and walnuts, and stir.

Preheat oven to moderate, 350°F. Butter a 2-quart soufflé dish.

Sprinkle the salt on the egg whites, and beat until stiff but not dry. Fold them into the yolk mixture carefully. Pour into soufflé dish. Place in shallow pan of hot water. Bake 35 minutes.

Serve at once.

This is an extremely sweet dessert, and is appropriate after a rather light main course. Serving this soufflé with Brandied Whipped Cream will accentuate the soufflé's flavor, and cut the sweetness, see page 230.

Yogi Liqueur Soufflé

[4 servings]

8 ladyfingers
½ cup brandy, or any cordial
4 tbsp. butter
2 tbsp. cornstarch
1 cup light cream, scalded
4 egg yolks
¼ cup sugar
5 egg whites

Soak the ladyfingers in ¼ cup of the brandy or cordial while preparing the soufflé mixture.

Melt the butter in a saucepan, stir in cornstarch and cook until smooth and bubby, about 2 minutes. Stir cream in, and cook for 5 minutes more, stirring constantly. Let cool for 5 minutes. Beat the egg yolks in a bowl until light in color. Gradually add the cream mixture, beating constantly to prevent curdling. Add sugar and the remaining brandy or cordial, and beat well together.

Preheat oven to moderate, 350°F. Butter a 1½-quart soufflé dish and dust with sugar.

Beat the egg whites until stiff but not dry. Fold them into the previous mixture. Pour half of the soufflé into the dish. Drain the ladyfingers and place them on the soufflé, pour rest of mixture on ladyfingers. Sprinkle a little sugar on top. Bake 30 minutes.

Serve at once.

Wine-Meringue Soufflé

[4 to 6 servings]

¾ cup vanilla wafer or cake crumbs
⅓ cup white wine
4 tbsp. butter
6 egg yolks, beaten
5 tbsp. sugar
5 egg whites

Soak the crumbs in the wine until saturated. Cream butter and egg yolks together until smooth. Combine the crumbs with the sugar, and add to the yolk mixture. Preheat oven to moderate, 375°F.

Beat the egg whites until stiff but not dry. Fold them into the crumb mixture carefully. Pour into a 2-quart soufflé dish. *Cover,* place in oven.

Bake for 30 minutes; prepare the following meringue to be placed on the soufflé at the end of that time:

3 egg whites
¼ cup sugar
2 tbsp. ground almonds

Beat the egg whites until stiff but not dry. Add sugar slowly, and mix well.

Open the oven, pull the soufflé to the opening but do not remove it from the oven. Place the meringue on top of the soufflé, and sprinkle almonds over the top. Do this all as quickly as possible. Do not cover. Increase the oven temperature to hot, 450°F. Bake an additional 5 minutes, or until meringue is lightly browned.

Serve at once.

EIGHT

Low-Calorie Soufflés

Diets are so dull—eggs, broiled meats, dry salads, and the like! It's no wonder that most people give up their diets sooner than they had planned. The recipes which follow are intended to provide soufflés with low-calorie counts, so that even the dieter may eat them.

If you will remember that an apple has 100 calories, you will be pleased to note that practically all the soufflés have about 100 calories (or even less) per serving. The dessert soufflés are particularly satisfying, because the average dieter misses something sweet in his meal. The flavors and textures of these soufflés are not too different from non-diet soufflés, so both dieters and non-dieters may enjoy them.

Just one word of caution: As there is no thickening agent in the low-calorie soufflés, they are apt to fall rather quickly.

So, serve at once!

Bacon-and-Tomato Soufflé

[4 servings; 95 calories per serving]

2 strips lean bacon	½ tsp. salt
1 tomato	⅛ tsp. pepper
4 egg yolks	4 egg whites

Broil bacon until crisp. Drain on absorbent paper. Set aside to cool. Cube the tomato, place in saucepan without water over low heat, and cook 5 minutes, stirring occasionally. Set aside to cool for 10 minutes.

Beat the egg yolks until thick. Add salt and pepper. Crumble the bacon into the yolks, and add the tomato. Stir well. Preheat oven to moderate, 350°F.

Beat the egg whites until stiff but not dry. Fold them into the yolk mixture carefully. Pour into an unbuttered 1-quart soufflé dish. Place the dish in a shallow pan of hot water. Bake 25 minutes.

Serve at once.

This soufflé makes an excellent lunch, particularly when served with a green salad.

Brunswick Soufflé

[4 servings; 100 calories per serving]

- 3 egg yolks
- ½ cup condensed cream of corn soup
- ½ cup finely chopped cooked chicken
- 3 egg whites
- 1 pimiento, sliced thin

Beat the egg yolks until thick. Add corn soup and chicken, mixing well. Correct the seasoning. Preheat oven to moderate, 350°F.

Beat the egg whites until stiff but not dry. Fold them into the corn mixture carefully. Pour the mixture into an unbuttered 1-quart soufflé dish. Place pimiento slices on top. Set the dish in a shallow pan of hot water. Bake 30 minutes.

Serve at once.

This soufflé makes an interesting and satisfying dinner.

Crab-Meat Soufflé

[4 servings; 100 calories per serving]

- ½ pound cooked crab meat, fresh or canned
- 2 tbsp. grated onion
- 1 tbsp. bread crumbs
- 2 tbsp. chopped parsley
- 1 minced pimiento
- 1 tsp. salt
- ¼ tsp. pepper
- 4 egg yolks
- 4 egg whites

Shred the crab meat and remove fibers, add onion, bread crumbs, parsley, and pimiento; mix well. Add salt and pepper to the egg yolks and beat until light in color. Combine well with the crab-meat mixture. Preheat oven to moderate, 350°F.

Beat the egg whites until stiff but not dry. Fold them into the crab-meat mixture carefully. Pour into an unbuttered 1-1½-quart soufflé dish. Place in a shallow pan of hot water. Bake 30 minutes.

Serve at once.

Cauliflower Soufflé

[4 servings; 115 calories per portion*]

1 medium-size head cauliflower
3 cups water
1 tsp. salt
2 tbsp. lemon juice
1 tbsp. butter *or* margarine, melted (optional)*
1/8 tsp. pepper
4 egg yolks
4 egg whites

Wash the cauliflower thoroughly; remove any discolored or bruised portions; separate into flowerets; discard the stem. Combine water, salt, lemon juice, and cauliflower. Cook until tender, about 15 minutes; drain. Force cauliflower through a sieve. Add butter (if desired) and pepper, and mix well. Let cool for 5 minutes.

Beat the egg yolks until light in color. Gradually add the cauliflower, beating constantly to prevent curdling. Correct seasoning. Set aside to cool for 10 minutes. Preheat oven to moderate, 375°F.

Beat the egg whites until stiff but not dry. Fold them carefully into the cauliflower mixture. Pour into an unbuttered 1-quart soufflé dish. Place in a shallow pan of hot water. Bake 25 minutes.

Serve at once.

* With the butter, this soufflé contains about 115 calories per portion. Without the butter, there are only 90 calories per portion.

Escarole Soufflé

[4 servings; 100 calories per serving]

- 2 cups broken escarole, lettuce, *or* endive, uncooked
- 1 tbsp. butter or margarine
- ½ cup water
- 1 tsp. salt
- ½ tsp. pepper
- 3 egg yolks, beaten
- 2 tbsp. grated Parmesan cheese
- 3 egg whites

Wash vegetable, drain. Add to butter and water in a saucepan. Season with the salt and pepper. Simmer over low heat for 10 minutes. Drain. Force the vegetable through a sieve. Set aside to cool for 10 minutes. Add the egg yolks gradually, mixing well. Add the cheese. Mix together. Preheat oven to moderate, 375°F.

Beat the egg whites until stiff but not dry. Fold them into the vegetable mixture carefully. Pour into an unbuttered 1-quart soufflé dish. Place the dish in a shallow pan of hot water. Bake 30 minutes.

Serve at once.

This is a rather bland soufflé, and should be served in place of a salad, or as an accompaniment to a meat course.

Mushroom Soufflé

[4 servings; 85 calories per serving]

1 tsp. butter *or* margarine	1 tsp. salt
1 cup chopped mushrooms	¼ tsp. pepper
2 tbsp. grated onion	3 egg yolks
1 tbsp. sifted all-purpose flour	3 egg whites

Melt butter in a saucepan, add mushrooms and onion. Sauté over low heat 5 minutes, stirring occasionally. Sprinkle with flour, salt, and pepper, and stir well. Cook 2 minutes more, stirring constantly. Set aside to cool for 15 minutes. Beat the egg yolks well. Add to the previous mixture, and beat until well blended. Preheat oven to moderate, 350°F.

Beat the egg whites until stiff but not dry. Fold them into the vegetable mixture carefully. Pour into an unbuttered 1-quart soufflé dish. Place in a shallow pan of hot water. Bake 25 minutes.

Serve at once.

Onion Soufflé

[4 servings; 90 calories per serving]

6 onions, peeled and sliced
1 cup water
2 tsp. salt
½ tsp. pepper
1 bay leaf
4 egg yolks
1 tsp. paprika
4 egg whites

Cook the onions in the water over low heat, with the salt, pepper, and bay leaf. When the onions are soft, about 20 minutes, drain and remove the bay leaf. Chop onions. Set aside to cool for 10 minutes. Beat the egg yolks until light in color; add paprika and pour into the onion mixture, beating well. Correct seasoning. Preheat oven to moderate, 350°F.

Beat the egg whites until stiff but not dry. Fold them into the onion mixture carefully. Pour into an unbuttered 1-1½-quart soufflé dish. Place in a shallow pan of hot water. Bake 30 minutes.

Serve at once.

Spinach Soufflé

[4 servings; 80 calories per serving]

- 2 cups cooked spinach
- 1 tsp. salt
- ¼ tsp. pepper
- 1 tbsp. grated onion
- 1 tsp. Worcestershire sauce
- 4 egg yolks
- 4 egg whites

Drain the spinach, chop, and combine with salt, pepper, onion and Worcestershire sauce, and stir well. (If spinach is hot, let cool for 10 minutes.) Beat the egg yolks until light in color, and add gradually to the spinach mixture, beating constantly. Preheat oven to moderate, 350°F.

Beat the egg whites until stiff but not dry. Fold them into the spinach mixture carefully. Pour into an unbuttered 1-1½-quart soufflé dish. Place the dish in a shallow pan of hot water. Bake 20 minutes.

Serve at once.

Tomato-and-Pea Soufflé

[4 servings; 90 calories per serving]

3 egg yolks
½ cup condensed tomato soup
⅔ cup canned peas, drained
3 egg whites

Beat the egg yolks in a bowl until thick. Add soup, and peas. Mix well. Correct the seasoning. Preheat oven to moderate, 350°F.

Beat the egg whites until stiff but not dry. Fold them into the tomato mixture carefully. Pour into an unbuttered 1-quart soufflé dish. Place in a shallow pan of hot water. Bake 30 minutes.

Serve at once.

This soufflé makes an excellent luncheon dish, or it may be served with a meat course.

Cream-of-Wheat Soufflé

[4 servings; 110 calories per serving]

1 cup skim milk
1 cup cooked Cream of Wheat *or* farina
½ tsp. salt
4 egg yolks
4 egg whites

Bring the milk to a boil, and add to the cooked cereal; stir well. It is important that no lumps remain. Force through a sieve to make the mixture smoother. Add salt, and stir. Let cool for 5 minutes. Beat the egg yolks until light in color. Add gradually to the cereal mixture, beating constantly to prevent curdling. Preheat oven to moderate, 350°F.

Beat the egg whites until stiff but not dry. Fold them into the cereal mixture carefully. Pour into an unbuttered 1-quart soufflé dish. Place the dish in a shallow pan of hot water. Bake 45 minutes.

Serve at once.

Rice Soufflé

[4 servings; 70 calories per serving]

1 cup cooked rice
1 tbsp. sugar
1 tbsp. grated orange rind
½ tsp. salt
5 egg whites
3 tbsp. dietetic jam or jelly*

Combine the rice, sugar, and orange rind in a saucepan, and stir together. (If the rice has not been cooked with salt, add salt now.) Preheat oven to moderate, 350°F.

Beat the egg whites until stiff but not dry. Fold them into the rice mixture carefully. Pour half the mixture into an unbuttered 1-quart soufflé dish. Spread jam or jelly lightly on top. Pour the remaining soufflé over the jelly. Place the dish in a pan of hot water. Bake 30 minutes.

Serve at once.

* If regular jam or jelly is used, this soufflé will contain 115 calories per serving.

NINE

Cold Soufflés

A cold soufflé in appearance resembles a hot soufflé—that is, it looks as if it had just risen in the oven, whereas it has only been in the refrigerator. This effect is achieved by overfilling the soufflé dish, so that when the soufflé mixture is thoroughly chilled, it will be set into place, higher than the level of the dish.

Be sure to use the size of soufflé dish specified in the following recipes, so that you will have enough mixture to pile high in the dish. Use a piece of waxed paper long enough to go around the outside edge of the dish, and fold it in half lengthwise. Butter the inside fold which is next to the soufflé mixture.

With string, tie the waxed paper, buttered side inside, around the soufflé dish, so that about 2 inches of the paper stands above the top of the dish. Cellophane tape may be used to hold the waxed paper firm, but it sometimes loosens; string is best. It should look like this:

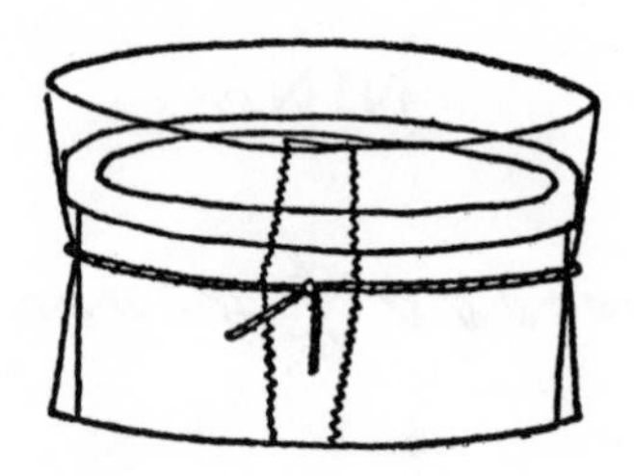

Pour the soufflé into the dish, filling dish and paper collar to 1½ inches above the top of the dish.

Set the soufflé in the refrigerator for chilling; make sure it has enough headroom, and is not touched by a refrigerator shelf. It should remain in the refrigerator for at least 4 hours, but more chilling is not harmful.

When ready to serve, remove dish from the refrigerator, cut the string holding the waxed paper. Remove the paper with care. Decorate the chilled soufflé with whipped cream, or other decorations called for in the recipe.

Cold Smoked-Salmon Soufflé

[4 to 6 servings]

- 1½ tbsp. gelatin
- ¼ cup cold water
- 2 tbsp. butter
- 2 tbsp. sifted all-purpose flour
- 1 cup milk, scalded
- 1 (3-oz.) package cream cheese, mashed
- ¼ tsp. black pepper
- 3 egg yolks, beaten
- ¼ lb. smoked salmon, minced
- ½ cup heavy cream, whipped
- 3 egg whites

Sprinkle the gelatin in the water; let soak while preparing the soufflé mixture.

Melt butter in a saucepan, stir in flour until smooth. Add milk, stirring constantly, until boiling point is reached. Cook over low heat 3 minutes, stirring occasionally. Remove from the heat. Add gelatin, and mix well until the gelatin is completely dissolved. Add cheese and pepper, and mix again. Add the egg yolks gradually, beating well. Let cool for 30 minutes. Add salmon and mix well. Add whipped cream, mixing lightly. Correct seasoning.

Butter a doubled strip of waxed paper, and tie it around the outside of a buttered 1-quart soufflé dish, so that the paper extends about 2 inches above the top of the dish.

Beat the egg whites until stiff but not dry. Fold them into the salmon mixture carefully. Pour soufflé mixture into the dish. Place in refrigerator for at least 4 hours. Remove collar carefully before serving. Serve soufflé as an appetizer.

Cold Chicken Soufflé

[6 servings]

3 tbsp. gelatin
½ cup cold water
1 cup hot chicken stock, *or* 1 chicken bouillon cube dissolved in 1 cup hot water
6 egg yolks
3 cups milk
2 cups ground cooked chicken
1 tsp. salt
½ tsp. pepper
1 cup heavy cream, whipped
3 egg whites

Sprinkle the gelatin in the water, and let soak for 5 minutes. Add stock, and stir until gelatin is completely dissolved. Let cool 15 minutes. Place over ice or cold water and beat with rotary beater for 5 minutes.

Beat the egg yolks in the top of a double boiler. Add the milk gradually, mixing well. Place over hot water, and cook, stirring constantly, until the mixture coats the spoon. Combine with the gelatin. Add the chicken, salt, and pepper, and mix well. Set aside to cool for 30 minutes. Add the whipped cream, mixing lightly.

Butter a doubled strip of waxed paper, and tie it around the outside of a 1-quart soufflé dish, so that the paper extends about 2 inches above the top of the dish.

Beat the egg whites until stiff but not dry and fold them into the chicken mixture carefully. Pour soufflé mixture into the dish. Place in refrigerator for at least 6 hours. Remove collar carefully. Decorate soufflé with pimiento strips, and serve with mayonnaise as a salad or serve with green salad as a main course.

Cold Ham Soufflé

[4 to 6 servings]

- 1½ tbsp. gelatin
- ¼ cup cold water
- 2 tbsp. butter
- 2 tbsp. sifted all-purpose flour
- 1 cup stock, *or* 1 cup hot water and 1 chicken bouillon cube
- 1 cup canned tomato sauce
- 2 egg yolks, beaten
- ¾ cup ground cooked ham
- 1 tbsp. sherry or Madeira
- 1½ cups heavy cream, whipped
- 2 egg whites

Sprinkle the gelatin in the water. Let soak while preparing the soufflé mixture.

Melt the butter in a saucepan, stir the flour in until smooth. Add stock and tomato sauce gradually, stirring constantly until boiling point is reached. Cook 3 minutes, stirring occasionally. Remove from the heat. Add the gelatin, and stir briskly until the gelatin is dissolved. Beat with a rotary beater for 5 minutes. Add the egg yolks gradually, beating constantly to prevent curdling. Add ham and sherry or Madeira, and stir well. Correct seasoning. Let cool for 30 minutes. Add the whipped cream, mixing gently.

Butter a doubled strip of waxed paper, and tie it around the outside of a buttered 1½-quart soufflé dish, so that the paper extends about 2 inches above the top of the dish.

Beat the whites until stiff but not dry. Fold them into the ham mixture carefully.

Pour soufflé mixture into the dish. Place in refrigerator for at least 6 hours. Remove collar carefully. Serve soufflé with a crisp green salad.

Cold Caramel Soufflé

[4 to 6 servings]

- ¾ cup sugar
- 1 tbsp. cornstarch
- ¾ cup water
- 2 tbsp. gelatin
- 2 tbsp. lemon juice
- 6 eggs
- ½ cup heavy cream, whipped

Mix ½ cup of the sugar with the cornstarch and ¼ cup of water, place over low heat; stir constantly until the sugar is dissolved. Continue to cook without stirring until the mixture turns dark caramel color. Add ¼ cup of water, mix well, and set aside to cool for 5 minutes.

Soften the gelatin in the remaining ¼ cup of water in the upper part of a double boiler. Add lemon juice, place over hot water and stir until completely dissolved.

Butter a 1-quart soufflé dish. Butter a doubled piece of waxed paper, and tie around the top of the dish, so that it extends 2 inches above the top.

Beat the eggs until light, add the remaining ¼ cup of sugar, continuing to beat until stiff. Add the caramel mixture, and the gelatin, and mix well. Let cool for 30 minutes. Place over ice or cold water and beat with a rotary beater for 5 minutes. Fold in the whipped cream. Pour the caramel mixture into the dish. Place in the refrigerator for at least 4 hours.

Remove paper, and decorate the soufflé with whipped cream.

Cold Chocolate Soufflé

[6 servings]

3 whole eggs
3 egg yolks
¼ cup sugar
3 oz. sweet chocolate
2 tbsp. brewed coffee
2 tbsp. gelatin
2 tbsp. cold water
1 cup heavy cream, whipped

Beat the whole eggs and the egg yolks together in the top of a double boiler. When light, add sugar and continue beating until thick. Place over hot water, and beat until thick and foamy. Melt chocolate in the coffee over low heat. Do not let boil. Set aside to cool for 10 minutes.

Butter a piece of waxed paper, and tie around the top of a buttered 1-quart soufflé dish. The paper collar should extend about 2 inches above the dish.

Soak gelatin in the cold water for 5 minutes. Place over hot water and stir until dissolved. Add the melted chocolate and gelatin to the egg mixture, and stir together carefully. Let cool for 30 minutes. Beat with a rotary beater for 5 minutes. Fold in the whipped cream slowly and gently.

Pour the soufflé into the dish. Chill in refrigerator at least 4 hours.

Remove the collar carefully to serve. Top the soufflé with cream, or a hot Chocolate Sauce, see page 225.

Cold Christmas Soufflé

[6 to 8 servings]

12 slices fruitcake, ½-inch thick
½ cup brandy
2 cups milk
1 cup light cream
4 eggs
¼ cup brown sugar (packed)
¼ cup granulated sugar
⅛ tsp. salt
¾ cup crumbled macaroons, *or* vanilla wafers

Soak the sliced fruitcake in the brandy, saturating each slice thoroughly. Let soak while preparing the soufflé mixture.

Scald the milk and cream together in a saucepan. Let cool for 15 minutes. Beat the eggs thoroughly; add the brown and white sugar, and the salt gradually. Beat well. Add the cooled milk and cream gradually, beating steadily. Preheat oven to moderate, 350°F.

Butter a 1½-quart soufflé dish, and place the soaked slices of cake in the bottom and around the sides of the dish. Spread the macaroon crumbs carefully over the slices of cake. Pour the milk mixture into the dish. Place in a shallow pan of hot water. Bake 40 minutes.

Remove from oven and let cool for 20 minutes; then place in refrigerator until thoroughly chilled, about 3 hours.

The soufflé may be unmolded, if desired, by running a knife around the edge and turning out onto a chilled plate. The soufflé may fall a little, but is still attractive and delicious.

Cold Brazilian Cottage-Cheese Soufflé

[6 to 8 servings]

- 1½ tbsp. gelatin
- ¼ cup cold strongly brewed coffee
- 1½ cups hot strongly brewed coffee
- ⅔ cup sugar
- 1½ cups creamed cottage cheese
- 2 egg yolks, beaten
- 3 tbsp. brandy
- 2 cups heavy cream
- 2 egg whites
- dash salt

Combine the gelatin with the cold coffee, and let soften for 5 minutes. Add hot coffee and sugar, and stir until gelatin is completely dissolved. Let cool for 30 minutes. Place over ice or cold water and beat with a rotary beater 5 minutes.

Force cheese through a sieve. Add the egg yolks and brandy, and beat thoroughly. Use electric or rotary mixer for at least 3 minutes. Add gelatin mixture and mix again. Whip the cream; fold into the cheese mixture.

Butter a 1-quart soufflé dish. Butter a doubled band of waxed paper, and tie it around the top of the soufflé dish, so that it extends about 2 inches above the edge.

Beat the egg whites with salt until stiff but not dry. Fold them into the cheese mixture carefully. Pour mixture into the soufflé dish. Place in a refrigerator for at least 4 hours. To serve, remove band carefully, and decorate the top with whipped cream.

Cold Grape-Juice Soufflé

[4 to 6 servings]

- 2 tbsp. gelatin
- ¼ cup cold unsweetened grape juice
- 2 cups hot unsweetened grape juice
- ¼ cup sugar
- 1 tbsp. lemon juice
- 4 egg whites
- dash salt

Combine the gelatin and cold grape juice. Let gelatin soften for 5 minutes. Stir in hot grape juice and sugar, and stir until the gelatin is dissolved. Add lemon juice. Set aside to cool for ½ hour, or until the mixture begins to thicken. Place over ice or cold water and beat with an electric mixer or rotary beater until thick and foamy.

Butter a 1-quart soufflé dish. Butter a doubled band of waxed paper, and tie around the top of the dish, so it extends about 2 inches above the edge.

Beat the egg whites and salt until stiff. Fold them into the grape-juice mixture carefully. Pour mixture into the soufflé dish. Place in the refrigerator for at least 4 hours. Remove paper band carefully before serving.

Cold Liqueur Soufflé

[6 to 8 servings]

- 5 egg yolks
- ½ cup sugar
- ¾ cup brandy
- ⅓ cup sherry
- 2 tbsp. lemon juice
- ¼ cup Benedictine *or* Chartreuse
- 2 tbsp. gelatin
- ½ cup water
- 5 egg whites
- 2 cups heavy cream, whipped

Beat the egg yolks until light. Add sugar gradually, beating until thick and light. Add brandy, sherry, lemon juice, and Benedictine or Chartreuse. Mix well.

Soak gelatin in water for 5 minutes. Place over hot water and stir until gelatin is dissolved. Add to the yolk mixture and mix well.

Prepare a 1½-quart soufflé dish by buttering and sprinkling with sugar. Butter a piece of doubled waxed paper, and tie it around the top of the dish, so as to form a collar standing about 2 inches above the top.

Beat the egg whites until stiff but not dry. Fold them into the gelatin mixture alternately with the whipped cream. Pour into the soufflé dish. Let chill at least 4 hours in the refrigerator. Remove collar carefully before serving.

Cold Mistletoe Soufflé

[4 to 6 servings]

6 egg yolks
¼ cup sugar
¼ cup lemon juice
1 tbsp. grated lemon rind
1 tbsp. gelatin
3 tbsp. cold water
1 cup heavy cream
3 tbsp. candied lemon peel

Beat the egg yolks in a bowl; add sugar gradually. Place the bowl over hot water, and continue beating about 3 minutes, or until the mixture is creamy. Remove from the hot water. Add lemon juice and rind, stir, and set aside.

Soak the gelatin in water for 5 minutes. Place over hot water and stir until gelatin is thoroughly dissolved. Add to the yolk mixture. Stir and set aside to cool for 30 minutes. When cooled, beat with a rotary beater for 5 minutes over ice water.

Butter a doubled piece of waxed paper and tie it around the top of a 1-quart soufflé dish, allowing it to stand 2 inches above the top.

Whip the cream until stiff, and fold it into the gelatin mixture. Pour soufflé into the dish. Place in refrigerator for at least 4 hours. Remove the paper carefully. Decorate the soufflé with candied lemon peel.

Cold Raspberry Soufflé

[4 to 6 servings]

½ cup sugar
1¼ cups water
2 cups raspberries, fresh or frozen
1 tbsp. gelatin
3 egg whites
1 cup heavy cream

Combine sugar and 1 cup water in a saucepan, and boil until syrupy, about 5 minutes. Add all but 2 tablespoons of the raspberries, and boil about 5 minutes. Force the berries through a sieve.

Soak gelatin in the remaining ¼ cup water. Place over hot water, and stir until gelatin is dissolved. Combine with the raspberry pulp, and mix well. Let cool for 30 minutes. Place over ice or cold water and beat with a rotary beater for 5 minutes.

Butter a doubled piece of waxed paper and tie it around the top of a buttered 1-quart soufflé dish, so that it stands about 2 inches above the top.

Beat the egg whites until stiff but not dry. Fold them into the raspberry mixture carefully. Whip the cream and fold into the berry mixture. Pour the mixture into the soufflé dish. Let it chill at least 4 hours in the refrigerator. Remove the band carefully.

Garnish the soufflé with whipped cream and the reserved whole raspberries.

TEN

Pudding Soufflés

The perfect soufflé is a light, fragile, and delicate creation. Its tiny pockets of air, which cause the soufflé to rise, also may cause it to fall when it cools. To search for a soufflé that will not fall after it is baked, is to find a dish that is not as light and delicate as a true soufflé should be.

As a compromise, the pudding soufflé has some merit. It is half pudding and half soufflé. It has the advantage, however, of being a dish that can be reheated.

If you make a pudding soufflé, and it is not eaten, you may return it to the oven much later (even after it has cooled completely), place it in a shallow pan of water, and it will rise again in about 20 or 30 minutes. The results, however, are never as spectacular as with a true soufflé.

For a busy person, who wishes to have her entire meal ready in advance, the pudding soufflé may be baked earlier in the day, removed from the oven, and then reheated at the last moment.

Coconut-and-Lemon Pudding-Soufflé

[4 servings]

3 tbsp. butter
⅜ cup sifted all-purpose flour
¾ cup milk, scalded
4 egg yolks
dash salt
3 tbsp. sugar
2 tbsp. lemon juice
2 tsp. grated lemon rind
½ cup grated coconut (dried, fresh, or frozen)
4 egg whites

Cream the butter until soft in a saucepan. Add flour, and continue creaming until well mixed. Add scalded milk, and place over low heat. Cook about 5 minutes, stirring constantly. The mixture should leave the sides of the pan. Remove from heat.

Beat the egg yolks with the salt until light in color; add sugar, lemon juice and rind. Combine with the butter mixture, beating steadily to prevent curdling. Let cool for 10 minutes.

Preheat oven to moderate, 350°F. Butter a 7-inch ring mold and dust with sugar.

Add coconut to the lemon mixture and stir well. Beat the egg whites until stiff but not dry. Fold them into the lemon mixture. Pour the soufflé into the mold. Place in a shallow pan of hot water. Bake 45 minutes.

When ready, remove from oven, and let settle for 2 minutes. Run a knife around the edge, tap the sides gently, and turn out carefully onto a warmed plate.

Serve at once.

Serve with Lemon Sauce, see page 227.

Mincemeat Pudding-Soufflé

[4 servings]

3 tbsp. butter
⅜ cup sifted all-purpose flour
¾ cup milk, scalded
4 egg yolks
3 tbsp. sugar
1 tsp. vanilla extract
½ cup finely ground mincemeat
4 egg whites

Cream the butter until soft in a saucepan. Add flour, and continue creaming until well mixed. Add scalded milk, and place over low heat. Cook 5 minutes, stirring constantly. The mixture should leave the sides of the pan. Remove from heat.

Beat the egg yolks until light in color; add sugar and vanilla, and beat together. Combine with the butter mixture, beating steadily to prevent curdling. Let cool for 10 minutes.

Preheat oven to moderate, 350°F. Butter a 7-inch ring mold, and dust with sugar.

Add mincemeat to the yolk mixture and stir well.

Beat the egg whites until stiff but not dry. Fold them into the mincemeat mixture. Pour the soufflé into the mold. Place in a shallow pan of hot water. Bake 45 minutes.

When ready, remove from oven, and let settle for 2 minutes. Run a knife around the edge, tap the sides gently, and turn out carefully onto a warmed plate.

Serve at once.

Serve with Vanilla Sauce, see page 229.

Vanilla Pudding-Soufflé

[4 servings]

- 4 tbsp. butter
- ½ cup sifted all-purpose flour
- 1 cup light cream, scalded
- 4 egg yolks
- ¼ cup sugar
- 1 tsp. vanilla extract
- 4 egg whites
- dash salt

Cream the butter until soft in a saucepan. Add flour, and continue creaming until it is well blended. Add cream, and place over low heat. Cook about 5 minutes, stirring constantly. The mixture should leave the sides of the pan. Remove from heat.

Beat the egg yolks until light in color; add sugar and vanilla, and beat together. Combine with the cream mixture, beating steadily to prevent curdling. Let cool for 10 minutes.

Preheat oven to moderate, 350°F. Butter a 7-inch ring mold thoroughly, and dust with sugar.

Beat the egg whites with salt until stiff, but not dry. Fold into the cream mixture carefully. Pour the soufflé into the mold. Place in a shallow pan of hot water. Bake 45 minutes.

When ready, remove from oven, and let settle for 2 minutes. Run a knife around the edge, tap the sides gently, and turn out carefully onto a warmed plate.

Serve at once.

Serve with Sabayon Sauce, see page 228.

ELEVEN

Soufflé Sauces

Tomato Vinaigrette Sauce

[1¼ cups]

- 1 cup of Tomato Sauce (page 231)
- ¼ cup tarragon vinegar
- 2 cloves garlic, minced
- 1 tsp. dry mustard
- 1 tsp. paprika
- ½ tsp. pepper
- 1 tsp. Worcestershire sauce
- 2 tbsp. boiling water
- 1 tbsp. butter

Heat the Tomato Sauce in a saucepan.

In another saucepan, combine vinegar, garlic, mustard, paprika, pepper, and Worcestershire sauce. Cook over low heat 5 minutes. Add Tomato Sauce, water, and butter. Mix well.

Serve hot with Eggplant Soufflé.

Mushroom Sauce

[1½ cups]

- 5 tbsp. butter
- 1 tbsp. minced onion
- 3 tbsp. sifted all-purpose flour
- 1½ cups milk, scalded
- ½ tsp. salt
- ½ cup chopped, uncooked mushrooms

Melt 3 tablespoons of the butter in a saucepan. Add onion, and cook 3 minutes over low heat. Stir flour in until smooth. Add milk gradually, stirring constantly, until boiling point is reached. Continue to cook over low heat 15 minutes, stirring occasionally. Add salt. Strain.

Melt the remaining 2 tablespoons of butter in a saucepan, add mushrooms and cook over medium heat 5 minutes. Combine with white sauce. Correct the seasoning.

Serve hot with Fish-Ball Soufflé.

Mushroom-Almond Sauce

[2 cups]

Add ½ cup toasted, blanched almonds to Mushroom Sauce.

Serve hot with Fish-Ring Soufflé, Calves'-Brain Soufflé.

Beef-Mushroom Sauce

[1½ cups]

- 6 tbsp. butter
- 2 tbsp. sifted all-purpose flour
- 2 cups beef stock, *or* 2 bouillon cubes dissolved in 2 cups hot water
- 1 cup sliced mushrooms, uncooked
- ½ tsp. salt
- 1 onion, peeled and chopped
- 1 tbsp. chopped parsley
- 1 tbsp. sherry

Melt 2 tablespoons of the butter in a saucepan and add flour. Cook, stirring constantly until the flour is well browned. Add stock gradually, stirring constantly, until boiling point is reached. Continue cooking over very low heat 30 minutes. Stir occasionally.

Melt the remaining butter in another saucepan. Add mushrooms, salt, onion, and parsley. Sauté 5 minutes, or until browned. Add sherry and 1 cup of the brown sauce. Cook 5 minutes, stirring occasionally.

Serve hot with Beef-Ring Soufflé or any vegetable soufflé.

Tomato Sauce

[2 cups]

3 tbsp. olive oil
1 onion, peeled and chopped
1 green pepper, chopped
1 (#2) can tomatoes
1 bay leaf
1 tsp. salt

Heat olive oil in a saucepan, add onion and green pepper. Cook, stirring constantly, until the onion begins to brown, about 3 minutes. Add tomatoes, bay leaf, and salt. Cook over low heat 45 minutes, stirring occasionally. Strain, pressing the tomato pulp through a sieve. Correct seasoning.

Serve hot with Cheese-and-Farina Soufflé, Hamburger Soufflé.

White Wine Sauce

[1¼ cups]

3 tbsp. white wine
¼ pound butter
4 egg yolks
¼ cup sliced mushrooms, sautéed
¼ cup chopped cooked shrimp
¼ tsp. salt
dash cayenne pepper
1 tsp. finely chopped parsley

Combine wine and butter in the top of a double boiler. Break butter into small pieces. Place over hot water and cook, stirring constantly until butter melts. Add 1 egg yolk at a time, beating constantly. Continue cooking, beating constantly, until sauce thickens. Remove from heat. Add the mushrooms, shrimp, salt, cayenne, and parsley. Mix well.

Serve hot with Finnan Haddie Soufflé.

Brown-Sugar Sauce

[1 cup]

¾ cup brown sugar (packed)
2 tbsp. sifted all-purpose flour
½ cup water
¼ cup fruit brandy (cherry, apricot, etc.)
1 tbsp. butter
2 tbsp. cream
½ tsp. vanilla extract
¼ cup chopped nuts (optional)

Combine sugar and flour in a saucepan. Add water and brandy, and stir until smooth. Cook, stirring constantly, until sugar dissolves and the mixture thickens, about 10 minutes. Add butter, cream, and vanilla. Stir until the butter melts. Add nuts if desired.

Serve warm with Apple Soufflé, Rice-Ring Soufflé, Sherry-Lemon Soufflé.

Caramel Sauce

[1¾ cups]

1 cup sugar
½ cup water
1 cup heavy cream
1 tsp. vanilla extract
dash salt

Combine sugar and water in a heavy pan. Cook, stirring constantly, until the sugar dissolves, and turns brown. Remove from heat. Add cream, vanilla, and salt. Mix well.

Serve hot or cold with Chestnut-Dessert Soufflé.

Chocolate Sauce

[⅔ cup]

3 squares (3 oz.) unsweetened chocolate
½ cup water
¼ cup sugar
dash salt
2 tbsp. butter
1 tsp. vanilla extract

Combine chocolate and water in a saucepan and cook over very low heat, stirring constantly until the chocolate melts. Add sugar and salt; cook, stirring constantly, until the mixture thickens. Add butter and vanilla. Mix well.

Serve warm with Banana Soufflé, Coffee Soufflé, Cream-Puff Soufflé, Cold Chocolate Soufflé.

Milk Chocolate Sauce

[⅔ cup]

½ cup powdered sugar
¼ cup cocoa
dash salt
¼ cup water
¼ cup light cream
½ tsp. vanilla extract

Sift the sugar, cocoa, and salt together into the top of a double boiler; stir the water and cream in gradually until smooth. Place over hot water; cook 20 minutes, stirring occasionally. Remove from heat and add vanilla.

Serve cold with Black-and-White Soufflé.

Coffee Sauce

[1½ cups]

3 egg yolks
¼ cup sugar
½ cup light cream
3 tbsp. brewed double-strength coffee
dash salt
½ tsp. vanilla extract
½ cup heavy cream, whipped

Beat the egg yolks lightly in the top of a double boiler. Add sugar, cream, coffee, and salt. Place over hot water, and cook, stirring constantly until smooth and thick, about 5 minutes. Add vanilla. Let cool thoroughly. Fold in the whipped cream.

Serve very cold with Chocolate-Bits Soufflé.

Foamy Sauce

[1½ cups]

2 egg yolks
1 cup confectioners' sugar
1 tsp. vanilla extract
½ cup heavy cream, whipped
2 egg whites

Beat the egg yolks in a bowl until light in color. Add sugar and vanilla gradually, beating constantly. Continue beating until thoroughly blended, and the mixture is light and frothy. Fold the whipped cream into the yolk mixture.

Beat the egg whites until stiff; fold them into the yolk mixture.

Serve cold with Chocolate-Tapioca Soufflé, Chocolate Soufflé, Fluffy Chocolate Soufflé.

Ginger Sauce

[¾ cup]

1½ tsp. powdered ginger
¼ cup sugar
¾ cup water
2 tsp. lemon juice
2 tbsp. brandy

Combine the ginger, sugar, and water in a saucepan. Cook, stirring constantly, until the sugar dissolves. Continue cooking, stirring frequently over low heat 15 minutes. Add lemon juice and brandy. Mix well.

Serve hot with Ginger and Candied-Fruit Soufflé.

Lemon Sauce

[1½ cups]

½ cup sugar
3 tbsp. sifted all-purpose flour
2 egg yolks, beaten
¾ cup cold water
1 tbsp. butter
⅔ cup lemon juice
2 tsp. grated lemon rind
¼ tsp. orange extract

Combine the sugar and flour in the top of a double boiler. Mix the egg yolks and water and add to the sugar mixture. Place over hot water, and cook 10 minutes, stirring constantly. Add butter, lemon juice, rind, and orange extract. Mix well.

This sauce may be served hot or cold with Avocado Soufflé, Lemon-Rind Soufflé, Coconut-and-Lemon Pudding Soufflé.

Raspberry Sauce

[1½ cups]

1 pint fresh raspberries, *or* 1 package frozen
¼ cup sugar
2 tbsp. cold water
⅛ tsp. orange extract

Wash and drain the berries. Crush with a spoon.

Combine sugar and water in a saucepan, and add the berries. Bring to a boil, and cook over very low heat 5 minutes, stirring occasionally. Force through a sieve. Add orange extract, and stir.

If desired, ½ cup whipped cream may be folded into the sauce.

Serve cold with Fresh Apricot Soufflé, Candied-Fruit Soufflé.

Sabayon Sauce

[¾ cup]

3 egg yolks
⅓ cup sugar
½ cup Marsala *or* Madeira wine
1 tbsp. brandy

Beat the egg yolks in the top of a double boiler. Add sugar gradually, beating well. Add the wine, a few drops at a time, stirring; place over lukewarm water. Cook, stirring constantly, until thick and creamy, but do not allow to boil. Add the brandy slowly, stirring.

Serve at once with Vanilla Pudding-Soufflé.

Strawberry Sauce

[1¾ cups]

3 tbsp. butter
1 cup powdered sugar
1 egg white
1 tbsp. brandy
1 cup crushed strawberries

Cream sugar and butter together until well blended.

Beat egg white until stiff. Fold the sugar mixture into the egg white. Add the brandy. Fold strawberry pulp in carefully.

Serve cold with Cream-Cheese Soufflé.

Vanilla Sauce

[3 cups]

4 egg yolks
1 cup sifted all-purpose flour
½ cup sugar
2 cups light cream, scalded
½ tsp. vanilla extract
¼ cup heavy cream, whipped

Beat the egg yolks in the top of a double boiler. Stir flour and sugar in and mix well. Add the cream gradually, beating constantly. Cook over hot water, stirring constantly until mixture coats the spoon, about 5 minutes. Add vanilla; let cool for 15 minutes. Fold in the whipped cream.

Serve cold with Strawberry Soufflé, Mincemeat Pudding-Soufflé.

Whipped Cream

[2 cups]

1 cup heavy cream
1 tbsp. sugar
½ tsp. vanilla extract

Whip the cream in a cold bowl until stiff. Add sugar and vanilla, and beat for an additional few turns of the beater. Do not overbeat.

Almond Whipped Cream

Add ¾ teaspoon almond extract (in place of vanilla). Add 2 tablespoons ground almonds to Whipped Cream above.

Fruit Whipped Cream

Make Whipped Cream, as described in recipe. Add ¼ cup mashed raw fruits, and 1 additional tablespoon of sugar. Fold in carefully.

Brandied Whipped Cream

Make Whipped Cream, as described in recipe. Add 2 tablespoons of brandy (or other liqueur) and beat for a few additional turns of the beater.

Serve with Baked-Apple Soufflé, Canned-Fig Soufflé, Hazelnut Soufflé, Walnut-and-Butterscotch Soufflé.

A Few Simple Cooking Definitions

Bake	To cook, by means of dry heat, in an oven.
Beat	To mix thoroughly, using a fork, wire whisk, rotary beater, or electric beater.
Blanch	To put boiling water over any food, particularly almonds, followed by immersion in cold water, to assist in the removal of the skins.
Blend	The combining of various ingredients by mixing smoothly together.
Boil	To heat a liquid or mixture until the surface bubbles and vapor rises.
Bouillon	A clear soup, made from fish, fowl, or meat.
Braise	To cook quickly in a little fat until brown, then reduce heat, and simmer in a covered pan with very little liquid.
Brush	To spread with melted butter or other liquid seasoning or coating.
Chop	To cut into small pieces with chopping knife.
Combine	The adding of one or more ingredients to another.
Cream	To soften ingredients by beating with a spoon into a smooth mixture of creamy texture.
Cube	To cut food in small cubes.
Dissolve	To liquefy or melt.

Dust	To sprinkle lightly with flour, sugar, or other dry coating.
Flake	To separate chunks of fish, crab, or other foods gently with a fork.
Fold in	To combine ingredients gently in horigontal folding action so as not to cause any loss of air.
Grate	To rub a food on a grater to reduce it to small pieces.
Grind	To put ingredients through a food mill or grinder.
Melt	To heat until the ingredient is liquefied.
Mince	To chop an ingredient as fine as possible.
Mix	To stir or beat foods together.
Parboil	To cook foods until partially cooked.
Purée	To press ingredients through a sieve or ricer. Also, the result of doing so.
Sauté	To cook over low heat in butter, oil or other fat.
Scald	To add boiling liquid to raw foods as aid in preparation. Also, to heat a liquid to the boiling point.
Sieve	Device or utensil, customarily having small holes which permit liquids or small particles to go through.
Sift	To separate the large particles from the small by employing a sieve, thus removing any lumps.
Simmer	To cook below, or just at, the boiling point.
Soak	To keep an ingredient covered with liquid as an aid in preparation.
Stir	To mix ingredients with a circular motion.
Stock	Broth made by long, slow cooking of veal or beef knuckle, chicken or other fowl, with vegetables, herbs, and seasonings. Strained and used as soup or sauce base.
Whip	To increase the volume of an ingredient by beating air into it.

Measures and Equivalents

A dash	=	Less than ⅛ teaspoon
3 teaspoons	=	1 tablespoon
2 tablespoons	=	1 fluid ounce
4 tablespoons	=	¼ cup
16 tablespoons	=	1 cup
2 cups	=	1 pint
4 cups	=	1 quart
6 cups	=	1½ quarts
8 cups	=	2 quarts

CANNED GOODS

8-ounce can	=	8 ounces	=	1 cup
No. 1 can*	=	11 ounces	=	1⅓ cups
No. 1½ can	=	16 ounces	=	2 cups
No. 2 can	=	20 ounces	=	2½ cups
No. 2½ can	=	28 ounces	=	3½ cups
No. 3 can	=	33 ounces	=	4 cups

* Some No. 1 cans contain 16 ounces, or 2 cups.

FOOD EQUIVALENTS

Apricots, dried	1 cup	= 1/3 pound
Butter	1 hotel bar	= 1/4 cup
Butter	1/4 cup	= 1/2 cup *or* 8 tablespoons
Chocolate, unsweetened	1 square	= 1 ounce
Cheese, American (grated)	1 cup	= 1/5 pound
Cheese, cottage	1 cup	= 1/2 pound
Cheese, cream	6 2/3 tablespoons	= 1 3-ounce package
Cheese, Parmesan (grated)	1 cup	= 1/4 pound
Cornstarch	1 tablespoon	= 2 tablespoons flour when used as a thickening agent)
Cream, heavy	1 cup	= 2 cups whipped cream
Dates, pitted	1 cup	= 1/2 pound
Graham crackers (crumbled)	9 or 10	= 1 cup
Lemon	1 large	= 3 to 4 tablespoons lemon juice
Lemon	1 large	= 1 1/2 teaspoons grated lemon rind
Macaroni, uncooked	1 cup	= 1/3 pound, uncooked
Macaroni, uncooked	1/2 cup	= 1 cup cooked maraconi

Nuts, chopped	1 cup	= ¼ pound
Orange	1 large	= ½ cup orange juice
Orange	1 large	= 1 tablespoon grated orange rind
Rice, uncooked	¼ cup	= 1 cup cooked rice
Sugar, brown	1⅛ cups, packed	= ½ pound
Sugar, white	1⅛ cups	= ½ pound
Vanilla wafers (crumbled) ..	24 to 30	= 1 cup
Zwieback (crumbled)	8 or 9	= 1 cup

Index

A CATALOG OF SELECTED

DOVER BOOKS

IN ALL FIELDS OF INTEREST

THE BOOK OF BEASTS: Being a Translation from a Latin Bestiary of the Twelfth Century, T. H. White. Wonderful catalog real and fanciful beasts: manticore, griffin, phoenix, amphivius, jaculus, many more. White's witty erudite commentary on scientific, historical aspects. Fascinating glimpse of medieval mind. Illustrated. 296pp. 5⅜ × 8¼. (Available in U.S. only) 24609-4 Pa. $5.95

FRANK LLOYD WRIGHT: ARCHITECTURE AND NATURE With 160 Illustrations, Donald Hoffmann. Profusely illustrated study of influence of nature—especially prairie—on Wright's designs for Fallingwater, Robie House, Guggenheim Museum, other masterpieces. 96pp. 9¼ × 10¾. 25098-9 Pa. $7.95

FRANK LLOYD WRIGHT'S FALLINGWATER, Donald Hoffmann. Wright's famous waterfall house: planning and construction of organic idea. History of site, owners, Wright's personal involvement. Photographs of various stages of building. Preface by Edgar Kaufmann, Jr. 100 illustrations. 112pp. 9¼ × 10.
23671-4 Pa. $7.95

YEARS WITH FRANK LLOYD WRIGHT: Apprentice to Genius, Edgar Tafel. Insightful memoir by a former apprentice presents a revealing portrait of Wright the man, the inspired teacher, the greatest American architect. 372 black-and-white illustrations. Preface. Index. vi + 228pp. 8¼ × 11. 24801-1 Pa. $9.95

THE STORY OF KING ARTHUR AND HIS KNIGHTS, Howard Pyle. Enchanting version of King Arthur fable has delighted generations with imaginative narratives of exciting adventures and unforgettable illustrations by the author. 41 illustrations. xviii + 313pp. 6⅛ × 9¼. 21445-1 Pa. $5.95

THE GODS OF THE EGYPTIANS, E. A. Wallis Budge. Thorough coverage of numerous gods of ancient Egypt by foremost Egyptologist. Information on evolution of cults, rites and gods; the cult of Osiris; the Book of the Dead and its rites; the sacred animals and birds; Heaven and Hell; and more. 956pp. 6⅛ × 9¼.
22055-9, 22056-7 Pa., Two-vol. set $21.90

A THEOLOGICO-POLITICAL TREATISE, Benedict Spinoza. Also contains unfinished *Political Treatise*. Great classic on religious liberty, theory of government on common consent. R. Elwes translation. Total of 421pp. 5⅜ × 8½.
20249-6 Pa. $6.95

INCIDENTS OF TRAVEL IN CENTRAL AMERICA, CHIAPAS, AND YUCATAN, John L. Stephens. Almost single-handed discovery of Maya culture; exploration of ruined cities, monuments, temples; customs of Indians. 115 drawings. 892pp. 5⅜ × 8½. 22404-X, 22405-8 Pa., Two-vol. set $15.90

LOS CAPRICHOS, Francisco Goya. 80 plates of wild, grotesque monsters and caricatures. Prado manuscript included. 183pp. 6⅝ × 9⅜. 22384-1 Pa. $4.95

AUTOBIOGRAPHY: The Story of My Experiments with Truth, Mohandas K. Gandhi. Not hagiography, but Gandhi in his own words. Boyhood, legal studies, purification, the growth of the Satyagraha (nonviolent protest) movement. Critical, inspiring work of the man who freed India. 480pp. 5⅜ × 8½. (Available in U.S. only)
24593-4 Pa. $6.95

ILLUSTRATED DICTIONARY OF HISTORIC ARCHITECTURE, edited by Cyril M. Harris. Extraordinary compendium of clear, concise definitions for over 5,000 important architectural terms complemented by over 2,000 line drawings. Covers full spectrum of architecture from ancient ruins to 20th-century Modernism. Preface. 592pp. 7½ × 9⅝. 24444-X Pa. $14.95

THE NIGHT BEFORE CHRISTMAS, Clement Moore. Full text, and woodcuts from original 1848 book. Also critical, historical material. 19 illustrations. 40pp. 4⅝ × 6. 22797-9 Pa. $2.50

THE LESSON OF JAPANESE ARCHITECTURE: 165 Photographs, Jiro Harada. Memorable gallery of 165 photographs taken in the 1930's of exquisite Japanese homes of the well-to-do and historic buildings. 13 line diagrams. 192pp. 8⅝ × 11¼. 24778-3 Pa. $8.95

THE AUTOBIOGRAPHY OF CHARLES DARWIN AND SELECTED LETTERS, edited by Francis Darwin. The fascinating life of eccentric genius composed of an intimate memoir by Darwin (intended for his children); commentary by his son, Francis; hundreds of fragments from notebooks, journals, papers; and letters to and from Lyell, Hooker, Huxley, Wallace and Henslow. xi + 365pp. 5⅜ × 8. 20479-0 Pa. $5.95

WONDERS OF THE SKY: Observing Rainbows, Comets, Eclipses, the Stars and Other Phenomena, Fred Schaaf. Charming, easy-to-read poetic guide to all manner of celestial events visible to the naked eye. Mock suns, glories, Belt of Venus, more. Illustrated. 299pp. 5¼ × 8¼. 24402-4 Pa. $7.95

BURNHAM'S CELESTIAL HANDBOOK, Robert Burnham, Jr. Thorough guide to the stars beyond our solar system. Exhaustive treatment. Alphabetical by constellation: Andromeda to Cetus in Vol. 1; Chamaeleon to Orion in Vol. 2; and Pavo to Vulpecula in Vol. 3. Hundreds of illustrations. Index in Vol. 3. 2,000pp. 6⅛ × 9¼. 23567-X, 23568-8, 23673-0 Pa., Three-vol. set $37.85

STAR NAMES: Their Lore and Meaning, Richard Hinckley Allen. Fascinating history of names various cultures have given to constellations and literary and folkloristic uses that have been made of stars. Indexes to subjects. Arabic and Greek names. Biblical references. Bibliography. 563pp. 5⅜ × 8½. 21079-0 Pa. $7.95

THIRTY YEARS THAT SHOOK PHYSICS: The Story of Quantum Theory, George Gamow. Lucid, accessible introduction to influential theory of energy and matter. Careful explanations of Dirac's anti-particles, Bohr's model of the atom, much more. 12 plates. Numerous drawings. 240pp. 5⅜ × 8½. 24895-X Pa. $4.95

CHINESE DOMESTIC FURNITURE IN PHOTOGRAPHS AND MEASURED DRAWINGS, Gustav Ecke. A rare volume, now affordably priced for antique collectors, furniture buffs and art historians. Detailed review of styles ranging from early Shang to late Ming. Unabridged republication. 161 black-and-white drawings, photos. Total of 224pp. 8⅜ × 11¼. (Available in U.S. only) 25171-3 Pa. $12.95

VINCENT VAN GOGH: A Biography, Julius Meier-Graefe. Dynamic, penetrating study of artist's life, relationship with brother, Theo, painting techniques, travels, more. Readable, engrossing. 160pp. 5⅜ × 8½. (Available in U.S. only) 25253-1 Pa. $3.95

HOW TO WRITE, Gertrude Stein. Gertrude Stein claimed anyone could understand her unconventional writing—here are clues to help. Fascinating improvisations, language experiments, explanations illuminate Stein's craft and the art of writing. Total of 414pp. 4⅜ × 6⅜. 23144-5 Pa. $5.95

ADVENTURES AT SEA IN THE GREAT AGE OF SAIL: Five Firsthand Narratives, edited by Elliot Snow. Rare true accounts of exploration, whaling, shipwreck, fierce natives, trade, shipboard life, more. 33 illustrations. Introduction. 353pp. 5⅜ × 8½. 25177-2 Pa. $7.95

THE HERBAL OR GENERAL HISTORY OF PLANTS, John Gerard. Classic descriptions of about 2,850 plants—with over 2,700 illustrations—includes Latin and English names, physical descriptions, varieties, time and place of growth, more. 2,706 illustrations. xlv + 1,678pp. 8½ × 12¼. 23147-X Cloth. $75.00

DOROTHY AND THE WIZARD IN OZ, L. Frank Baum. Dorothy and the Wizard visit the center of the Earth, where people are vegetables, glass houses grow and Oz characters reappear. Classic sequel to *Wizard of Oz*. 256pp. 5⅜ × 8. 24714-7 Pa. $4.95

SONGS OF EXPERIENCE: Facsimile Reproduction with 26 Plates in Full Color, William Blake. This facsimile of Blake's original "Illuminated Book" reproduces 26 full-color plates from a rare 1826 edition. Includes "The Tyger," "London," "Holy Thursday," and other immortal poems. 26 color plates. Printed text of poems. 48pp. 5¼ × 7. 24636-1 Pa. $3.50

SONGS OF INNOCENCE, William Blake. The first and most popular of Blake's famous "Illuminated Books," in a facsimile edition reproducing all 31 brightly colored plates. Additional printed text of each poem. 64pp. 5¼ × 7. 22764-2 Pa. $3.50

PRECIOUS STONES, Max Bauer. Classic, thorough study of diamonds, rubies, emeralds, garnets, etc.: physical character, occurrence, properties, use, similar topics. 20 plates, 8 in color. 94 figures. 659pp. 6⅛ × 9¼. 21910-0, 21911-9 Pa., Two-vol. set $15.90

ENCYCLOPEDIA OF VICTORIAN NEEDLEWORK, S. F. A. Caulfeild and Blanche Saward. Full, precise descriptions of stitches, techniques for dozens of needlecrafts—most exhaustive reference of its kind. Over 800 figures. Total of 679pp. 8⅛ × 11. Two volumes. Vol. 1 22800-2 Pa. $11.95
Vol. 2 22801-0 Pa. $11.95

THE MARVELOUS LAND OF OZ, L. Frank Baum. Second Oz book, the Scarecrow and Tin Woodman are back with hero named Tip, Oz magic. 136 illustrations. 287pp. 5⅜ × 8½. 20692-0 Pa. $5.95

WILD FOWL DECOYS, Joel Barber. Basic book on the subject, by foremost authority and collector. Reveals history of decoy making and rigging, place in American culture, different kinds of decoys, how to make them, and how to use them. 140 plates. 156pp. 7⅞ × 10¾. 20011-6 Pa. $8.95

HISTORY OF LACE, Mrs. Bury Palliser. Definitive, profusely illustrated chronicle of lace from earliest times to late 19th century. Laces of Italy, Greece, England, France, Belgium, etc. Landmark of needlework scholarship. 266 illustrations. 672pp. 6⅛ × 9¼. 24742-2 Pa. $14.95

ILLUSTRATED GUIDE TO SHAKER FURNITURE, Robert Meader. All furniture and appurtenances, with much on unknown local styles. 235 photos. 146pp. 9 × 12. 22819-3 Pa. $7.95

WHALE SHIPS AND WHALING: A Pictorial Survey, George Francis Dow. Over 200 vintage engravings, drawings, photographs of barks, brigs, cutters, other vessels. Also harpoons, lances, whaling guns, many other artifacts. Comprehensive text by foremost authority. 207 black-and-white illustrations. 288pp. 6 × 9. 24808-9 Pa. $8.95

THE BERTRAMS, Anthony Trollope. Powerful portrayal of blind self-will and thwarted ambition includes one of Trollope's most heartrending love stories. 497pp. 5⅜ × 8½. 25119-5 Pa. $8.95

ADVENTURES WITH A HAND LENS, Richard Headstrom. Clearly written guide to observing and studying flowers and grasses, fish scales, moth and insect wings, egg cases, buds, feathers, seeds, leaf scars, moss, molds, ferns, common crystals, etc.—all with an ordinary, inexpensive magnifying glass. 209 exact line drawings aid in your discoveries. 220pp. 5⅜ × 8½. 23330-8 Pa. $4.50

RODIN ON ART AND ARTISTS, Auguste Rodin. Great sculptor's candid, wide-ranging comments on meaning of art; great artists; relation of sculpture to poetry, painting, music; philosophy of life, more. 76 superb black-and-white illustrations of Rodin's sculpture, drawings and prints. 119pp. 8⅜ × 11¼. 24487-3 Pa. $6.95

FIFTY CLASSIC FRENCH FILMS, 1912-1982: A Pictorial Record, Anthony Slide. Memorable stills from Grand Illusion, Beauty and the Beast, Hiroshima, Mon Amour, many more. Credits, plot synopses, reviews, etc. 160pp. 8¼ × 11. 25256-6 Pa. $11.95

THE PRINCIPLES OF PSYCHOLOGY, William James. Famous long course complete, unabridged. Stream of thought, time perception, memory, experimental methods; great work decades ahead of its time. 94 figures. 1,391pp. 5⅜ × 8½. 20381-6, 20382-4 Pa., Two-vol. set $19.90

BODIES IN A BOOKSHOP, R. T. Campbell. Challenging mystery of blackmail and murder with ingenious plot and superbly drawn characters. In the best tradition of British suspense fiction. 192pp. 5⅜ × 8½. 24720-1 Pa. $3.95

CALLAS: PORTRAIT OF A PRIMA DONNA, George Jellinek. Renowned commentator on the musical scene chronicles incredible career and life of the most controversial, fascinating, influential operatic personality of our time. 64 black-and-white photographs. 416pp. 5⅜ × 8¼. 25047-4 Pa. $7.95

GEOMETRY, RELATIVITY AND THE FOURTH DIMENSION, Rudolph Rucker. Exposition of fourth dimension, concepts of relativity as Flatland characters continue adventures. Popular, easily followed yet accurate, profound. 141 illustrations. 133pp. 5⅜ × 8½. 23400-2 Pa. $3.50

HOUSEHOLD STORIES BY THE BROTHERS GRIMM, with pictures by Walter Crane. 53 classic stories—Rumpelstiltskin, Rapunzel, Hansel and Gretel, the Fisherman and his Wife, Snow White, Tom Thumb, Sleeping Beauty, Cinderella, and so much more—lavishly illustrated with original 19th century drawings. 114 illustrations. x + 269pp. 5⅜ × 8½. 21080-4 Pa. $4.50